THE INDUSTRIAL REVOLUTION:

Technological and Social Change In Europe and the United States

BY DAVID GRABER

COPYRIGHT © 1995 Mark Twain Media, Inc.

ISBN 1-58037-082-9

Printing No. CD–1837

Mark Twain Media, Inc., Publishers
Distributed by Carson-Dellosa Publishing Company, Inc.

TABLE OF CONTENTS

TIME LINE

1733   John Kay invents the "flying shuttle."

1754   First iron-rolling mill—Hampshire, England.

1764   James Watt invents the condenser—first step to perfecting the steam engine.

1764   James Hargreaves invents the "jenny."

1776   Adam Smith publishes *Wealth of Nations*—philosophical basis for *laissez-faire* economics.

1776   American colonies begin revolt against English rule.

1784   Andrew Meikle invents the threshing machine.

1784   Henry Cort develops the puddling process for wrought iron

1785   James Watt installs a steam engine in a cotton-spinning factory.

1792   First illuminated gas lighting—England.

1793   Eli Whitney invents the cotton gin.

1794   First telegraph installed—Lille, France.

1800   Robert Owen opens a mill at New Lanarck, Scotland.

1811   Luddites protest loss of cottage industry jobs, destroy factory equipment in England.

1814   George Stephenson invents the first practical locomotive.

1830s   The first great railway building boom begins in Europe and the United States.

1833   British Factory Act—limits child labor and creates inspection process.

1834   Cyrus McCormick patents the reaping machine.

1840s   Pennsylvania, Massachusetts, and Connecticut pass laws limiting child labor. Child labor continues in other states.

1847   Karl Marx and Friedrich Engels publish *The Communist Manifesto*.

1850s   First chemical fertilizers developed.

1856   Henry Bessemer introduces the "Bessemer process" for steel production.

1858   Open hearth furnace first used for steel production.

1860   Joseph Lenoir invents the first practical internal combustion engine.

1861–1865   American Civil War.

1866   Alfred Nobel invents dynamite.

1869   Transcontinental railroad line completed—Promontory Point, Utah.

1869   Knights of Labor formed—first national American labor union.

1870   Europe begins its "Imperial Age."

1870   John D. Rockefeller forms Standard Oil Company.

1880   George Pullman builds his company town.

1882   Thomas Edison constructs first central power station to electrify New York City.

1884   London subway opened.

1884   Rayon invented—first synthetic clothing material.

1886   Aluminum produced for the first time.

1892   Andrew Carnegie forms Carnegie Steel Corporation.

1893   Workers strike at Pullman, Illinois. Strike broken by government troops.

1893   Henry Ford builds his first car.

1901   Beginning of the Progressive Era. Theodore Roosevelt becomes president when William McKinley is assassinated.

1901   Carnegie Steel sold to J.P. Morgan. Morgan forms U.S. Steel.

1903   Wright brothers complete first successful airplane flight.

1903   Henry Ford founds Ford Motor Company.

1908 Ford produces first Model T. Fifteen million eventually sold.

1909 Leo Baekeland produces the first plastic.

1914–1918 World War I.

1916 Beginning of Great Migration—African-Americans move north in search of work and a better life.

1917 Communist revolution in Russia.

1927 Ford produces the last Model T.

1928 Joseph Stalin—first Five-Year Plan begins Soviet industrialization.

1935 Franklin Roosevelt creates the Rural Electrification Administration to bring electricity to rural areas.

1938 Fair Labor Standards Act prohibits most forms of child labor in the United States.

1939–1945 World War II

1945 First atomic bomb dropped—Hiroshima, Japan.

INTRODUCTION

In 1867 English statesman Benjamin Disraeli noted, "Change is inevitable in a progressive society. Change is constant." Disraeli lived in a rapidly changing world. For centuries, however, technological change in Europe had been stagnant. The people lived and worked with the same simple tools that their ancestors had used. Little had changed in people's daily lives since the time of the Roman Empire 1,500 years before. As in the distant past, candles lit homes, animals provided traction for farmers, and craftsmen used their skills to fashion hand-constructed goods needed in the primitive economy. In the mid-1700s the changes began. While the American colonies revolted against their English king, an equally profound international revolution was beginning. Rather than a political revolution, this was a revolution of technological and social change, commonly called the Industrial Revolution.

The Industrial Revolution was a revolution of inventiveness. The changes started slowly but multiplied in number as the decades passed. Starting in England, inventors and businessmen combined their talents to create new means of production and to harness the power of machines. Life changed dramatically, both for better and worse, for the people of England. Dramatic social changes accompanied the technological changes. Old ways of living and working disappeared forever. Soon the new technologies spread beyond England's shores, and the revolution took hold throughout Europe and the United States. The age of the machine had begun.

BEFORE THE INDUSTRIAL REVOLUTION

Unlike political revolutions, the Industrial Revolution did not begin with great civil unrest or the clash of armies. As a result, it is difficult to arrive at a date for its beginning. The Industrial Revolution did not occur overnight, but rather began gradually and grew over several decades. Most historians place its beginnings in England in the mid-1700s, a decade or two before the American Revolution.

Prior to the Industrial Revolution, most people were involved in agriculture and cottage industry.

Most people lived in the country before the Industrial Revolution. In England, 75 percent of the population lived in rural areas or small villages in 1700. The percentage was even higher in continental Europe. Those cities that existed were few in number and of modest population. Due to the limited development of farming methods, it was necessary for the majority of the people to live in the country in order to produce enough food for the population. Most families farmed and lived on small plots of land that were controlled by large land owners who were often members of the nobility.

The total population of Europe was quite small. For example, in 1700 England's total population was about five million, compared to 70 million today. The people of preindustrial Europe lived very isolated lives. Roads were poor and dangerous, so people rarely traveled beyond their home villages. News of events in the outside world arrived slowly and sporadically. As a result, the small villages that dotted the countryside were the centers of life for the majority of Europeans. Few people ever left the area of their birth.

While the vast majority of the population worked in the fields, farming did not provide year-round employment. The peasant farmers were quite busy during times of planting and harvesting, but at other times they were free to do other work. During these times, thousands of families worked in their homes for clothing merchants. The merchants provided the families with wool or cotton, and for a fixed price, the families spun yarn on their spinning wheels and produced cloth on their hand-operated looms. This practice between the merchants and rural families is known as "cottage industry" because all of the work was done in a family's cottage home.

Weaving cloth was difficult and tedious, but provided a valuable income for many families. It was convenient work, since it was performed from within the home and at the pace desired by the worker. Children worked along with their parents, often becoming skilled at spinning yarn at a young age.

The system also had advantages for the merchants. The merchants paid very little for the cloth produced by the rural families and could then sell it at a handsome profit. However, the merchants were troubled by the inconsistent levels of production by the families and had no way to supervise their work. Often the cloth would not be delivered on time, especially when there was field work to divert the families from their spinning and weaving. Thus, the merchants desired another system that would allow greater supervision, more consistent delivery, and increased production. When the opportunity to produce their goods through new methods came, the merchants were quick to seize it.

Name_____ Date _____

POINTS TO PONDER

1. Cottage industry provided many advantages to both the merchants and to the workers. Who do you think benefited more from the cottage industry system? Why?

_____

_____

_____

_____

_____

2. What problems do you see with the cottage industry system? Would a similar system work well in today's world? Why or why not?

_____

_____

_____

_____

3. Before the Industrial Revolution, life was centered around small villages due to the difficulty of travel and limited communication with the outside world. While people were isolated from the outside world, they also spent their lives in a safe, familiar community. Would you prefer the community you live in now, or one more like a village before the Industrial Revolution? Give reasons for your answer.

_____

_____

_____

_____

_____

Name_____ Date_____

CHALLENGES

1. When do historians date the start of the Industrial Revolution?

_____

2. Why did most of the people live in the country before the Industrial Revolution?

_____

_____

3. What was England's population in 1700?

_____

4. Why were the European villages isolated?

_____

_____

5. Where did the term "cottage industry" get its name?

_____

_____

6. Why did rural families participate in cottage industry?

_____

_____

7. What advantages did cottage industry offer to the merchants?

_____

_____

8. What problems did the merchants face with cottage industry?

_____

_____

9. What goods were commonly produced by cottage industry?

_____

10. What was the primary occupation of most of the people involved with cottage industry?

_____

THE FIRST IMPORTANT INVENTIONS

Steam Engine

The cottage industry system had developed over a course of many centuries. Although minor improvements were made to speed up the process of making yarn and cloth, the procedures remained fundamentally the same until the mid-1700s. Then several English inventors produced devices that increased production but also brought about the demise of cottage industry.

The most time-consuming part of producing cloth was the spinning of the cotton into yarn. In 1700 it took approximately ten spinners to produce enough yarn to keep one weaver busy at her loom. In 1733 John Kay invented the "flying shuttle," a device that sped up the production of the weavers. This made the imbalance between spinning and weaving even greater. For years, people searched for ways to speed up the process of spinning yarn. In 1764 James Hargreaves invented a hand-operated device he called the "jenny." It allowed one person to spin eight threads at once; further improvements increased that number to as many as eighty threads. This was a great improvement, but it did not fundamentally change the nature of production. The device was still operated by hand and used in the peasant cottages.

It only took four more years for Hargreaves' invention to be dramatically improved upon. Richard Arkwright used many of the same ideas behind the "jenny" in his invention called the "water frame." As the name indicates, the machine was powered by water. Spinning mills, powered by waterwheels, were set up next to streams. Samuel Crompton further improved upon the water frame in 1787 when he invented a spinning machine called the "mule." It was powered by James Watt's newly perfected steam engine. These inventions were too large and required too much power to be practical in cottage homes. Therefore, cottage industry began to decline. The city of Manchester, England, became the center of textile production when there was a boom in factory construction there at the end of the eighteenth century. In 1782 Manchester had two factories, but by 1802 there were more than fifty, easily making Manchester the largest producer of textiles in the world. After 1820, weaving sheds that used Edmund Cartwright's power loom were often added to the spinning mills, bringing the entire process of fabric manufacturing to one location.

It was James Watt's perfection of the steam engine that provided the power to run the factories. Primitive and inefficient steam-powered engines had been used to pump water from coal mines for several decades, but Watt produced the first steam engine that was powerful and efficient enough to be used to provide power for industry. The invention of the steam engine allowed factories to end their dependence on the waterwheel and, thus, ended the need to be located next to streams or rivers. The steam engine was fueled by coal, making coal an increasingly important resource. It was difficult to transport large amounts of coal, so now it was important that factories be located near a cheap supply of coal.

The idea of textile factories soon spread beyond England to France, Belgium, Germany, and the United States as businessmen saw the advantages of factory production. Cottage industry was soon unable to compete with the factories. The Industrial Revolution had begun.

Name_____ Date_____

POINTS TO PONDER

1. The invention of power-driven machines and the factory system led to the end of cottage industry. What do you think happened to the people who depended on cottage industry for part of their incomes?

_____

_____

_____

_____

2. Inventors such as Watt, Crompton, and Cartwright created devices that dramatically changed people's lives. Can you think of recent inventions that have changed the way people live in your lifetime? List any you think are important.

_____

_____

_____

_____

_____

3. The steam engine was an important source of power for early factories. Today steam power is rarely used. What sources of power are commonly used today?

_____

_____

_____

_____

_____

Name _____ Date _____

CHALLENGES

1. What was the most time-consuming part of textile production?

_____

2. James Hargreaves' "jenny" was one of the first inventions we discussed. How did it improve the spinning process?

_____

_____

3. Richard Arkwright and Samuel Crompton also invented spinning machines. What were the machines called?

_____

_____

4. What English city became the center of textile production?

_____

5. What two sources of power were used to run a textile factory's machines?

_____

6. Where were primitive forms of the steam engine used before James Watt perfected it?

_____

_____

7. What fuel was used to run the steam engines?

_____

8. Name three of the countries that followed England's use of factories.

_____

_____

9. How did Watt's steam engine change the way factory locations were selected?

_____

_____

THE TEXTILE INDUSTRY

With the growth of the factory system, England experienced a huge increase in textile production. In the past, production had taken place in the cottages of the country. By the late 1700s new factories were being built in northern England that employed thousands of workers. The small factory towns grew into cities almost overnight.

England's new factory cities were dominated by the economic activity surrounding the textile mills. The new cities were poorly planned due to their rapid growth and soon became heavily polluted. They lacked sewers, paved streets, and safe water sup-

Workers lived in overcrowded, poorly planned neighborhoods.

plies. Workers lived in poorly constructed shacks in the crowded slums that grew up next to the factories. Of the new cities, Manchester was the largest and most important. Its population grew from 25,000 in 1770 to 450,000 in 1850. For a century, the city of Manchester was the leading producer of textile products.

The cities' populations were clearly divided into two new social groups: the mill owners and the workers. The mill owners were hard-working, aggressive men who were able to turn small investments into fortunes. They were often ruthless in their pursuit of profits. Unfortunately, most of them cared little about their workers, who lived in poverty. The mill owners became the wealthiest and most powerful people in the new industrial cities. The workers, however, made up the majority of the population. They often owned almost nothing other than the value of their labor. They lived in the worst sections of the city and constantly struggled to make enough money to survive. They often worked 14 or 16 hours a day in the textile mills for very low wages. Conditions in the mills were unhealthy. The air was filled with dust from the cotton, and the temperature was extremely hot in the summer and very cold in the winter. Accidents often occurred when exhausted workers fell asleep at their machines.

International trade was very important to the success of the factory system. The production of clothing and other cotton items increased dramatically with the use of the new machines. The English people bought much of the clothing that was produced, but didn't need all of it. Manufacturers needed new markets for their cotton goods. For many years, England had traded its products with other nations, and with the growth of the factory system, England's trade increased substantially. A large portion of England's textile production went to China, India, Africa, and other parts of the world that had not begun to industrialize.

England also needed to broaden its trade to insure sources of cotton. English farmers could not grow cotton because of the cold climate, so it had to be imported from other countries. At first most of the cotton came from the West Indian Islands, a colony of England. After 1800 more and more cotton came from the slave plantations of the southern United States. By 1840 England obtained three-fourths of its cotton from the United States.

Industrial cities grew in other European countries soon after they appeared in England. France, Belgium, and Germany soon saw their cities develop many of the same characteristics that Manchester had. However, none of these cities ever approached the level of production or degree of poverty for which Manchester was famous.

8

Name_____ Date _____

POINTS TO PONDER

1. The factory workers of Manchester lived in horrible slums. Slum areas are still a problem in today's modern cities. Why do you think we have not been able to eliminate the problems of poverty and slum areas in our cities?

_____

_____

_____

_____

2. Many early factory owners were ruthless in their pursuit of profit and obtained great riches while their workers lived in poverty. However, their risky investments were an essential part of developing the factory system that has benefited humanity. Do you think the contributions of the factory owners outweigh the damage caused by the exploitation of their workers?

_____

_____

_____

_____

_____

3. International trade was an important part of the early industrial economy. Trade between nations is even more important today. What products does the United States often import from other countries? What products do we often export to other countries?

_____

_____

_____

_____

_____

Name_____ Date _____

CHALLENGES

1. Why were the new factory cities poorly planned?

_____

_____

2. What were some characteristics of the new cities?

_____

_____

3. What two new social groups populated the growing cities?

_____

_____

4. What were some characteristics of the mill owners?

_____

_____

5. Describe working conditions in the factory.

_____

_____

6. Why was international trade important to the factory cities?

_____

_____

7. Name one of the places mentioned where England sold large portions of its textile production.

_____

8. From where did England import three-fourths of its cotton by 1840?

_____

9. What English city became the center of textile industry?

_____

10. Why did England have to import its raw cotton from other nations?

_____

_____

10

THE DEVELOPMENT OF MODERN AGRICULTURE

The invention of the steel plow allowed farmers to till heavy soils more easily and quickly than ever before.

Many people had moved to the city from farms to seek work in the growing factories. To provide these people with grains, vegetables, and meats, more food needed to be produced by a smaller percentage of the population.

England had the largest cities and the most developed industry in the nineteenth century, but it also had the most trouble with providing food to its growing cities. In preindustrial times the majority of the people were peasant farmers. By 1800, 36 percent of the labor force was involved in agriculture, and less than 7 percent of the labor force farmed by 1900. Other industrializing nations saw a similar reduction in the number of people involved in farming. New technologies and practices increased agricultural production and also reduced the need for farm laborers.

Many factors contributed to increased farm production. In England, new laws changed medieval practices that distributed land inefficiently among the population. Large landowners gained control of more of the land and were instrumental in bringing modern farming practices into use. The large landowners were more willing to try new methods of farming. They encouraged the use of new crops such as turnips and potatoes. Under their direction, new breeds of cattle and sheep were developed that produced more meat, were ready for slaughter at a younger age, and proved more resistant to disease. Horses replaced oxen to pull field implements such as plows. The practices of using the manure from animals to fertilize fields and using crop rotation methods became common. Landowners found that by changing the crops planted from year to year, the soil was able to recover its fertility. Swamps and marshes were also brought into production by using new drainage techniques.

Agriculture also benefited from many new inventions. Chemical fertilizers were developed in the 1850s and were soon widely used to increase the land's fertility. More iron and steel was used in tools and farm implements. Mechanical seed drills were used. Wooden plows were replaced by iron and then steel plows that broke less frequently and turned heavy soil much more easily. Steam-powered threshing machines and reapers began to appear in 1850. After 1900 the first tractors appeared and gradually replaced horses for field work. All of these machines reduced the need for human labor and increased the number of workers available to the factories.

Agriculture also played a role in supplying industry with raw materials. Vast amounts of cotton were needed to supply the textile mills of England. The southern United States had an ideal climate and soil for raising cotton. English textile industry imported most of its cotton from the United States after 1800. Cotton production required large amounts of labor and was raised on the large slave plantations of the southern states. After the American Civil War freed the slaves, cotton production continued in a share-cropping system.

The trend toward larger farms operated by fewer farmers continues up to the present day. The increased use of machinery, chemical fertilizers, and improved breeds of livestock have allowed modern farmers to produce more with less human labor than ever before.

Name_____ Date _____

POINTS TO PONDER

1. With the decline of the number of people needed to work on the farms, more people moved to the cities to find work. Do you think that most of the people made this move willingly? Why might they have preferred to stay in the country? Why would the city have been more appealing?

_____

_____

_____

_____

2. The early factory workers of the Industrial Revolution and the slaves on the southern cotton plantations both had very difficult lives. Both groups of people were victims of social attitudes and the nature of the economy. Can you think of any groups of people today who are suffering because of the way the economy is changing or because of opinions society has about them?

_____

_____

_____

_____

3. Agriculture has continued to evolve. New technologies are constantly being put into use and fewer farmers are needed to farm more land as machinery gets bigger. Are there any potential disadvantages to having a declining number of farmers? What does our culture lose with the loss of so many family farms?

_____

_____

_____

_____

Name_____ Date_____

CHALLENGES

1. What was the dilemma faced by agriculture as a result of the Industrial Revolution?

_____

_____

2. Of the industrialized countries, England had the smallest percentage of its population involved in agriculture. What percentage of England's people were farmers in 1900?

_____

3. What group of farmers were the most open to the idea of changing traditional farming practices and techniques?

_____

4. What new crops were widely used in the 1800s?

_____

_____

5. How were the new breeds of livestock better than the old breeds?

_____

_____

6. Name three new machines used by farmers.

_____

_____

7. Where was most cotton grown?

_____

8. What farming trends of the 1800s have continued to the present day?

_____

_____

9. How did farmers increase the fertility of their soil?

_____

_____

10. What system was used to continue cotton production in the United States after the Civil War?

_____

TRANSPORTATION: THE DOMINANCE OF THE RAILROADS

In 1769 James Watt produced the first efficient steam engine. It was only a matter of time until his invention was put to use as a power source for transporting goods. Steam power was first used on ships, powering river boats in the early 1800s. However, it was the steam locomotive that truly revolutionized transportation.

The completion of the transcontinental railroad opened up the American West for settlement and trade.

Primitive railroad tracks had long been used in mining operations. Carts were pushed along the tracks by men or pulled by horses. Railroad tracks were rarely used to travel long distances, however. Canals and rivers were used to transport most heavy goods. Unfortunately, rivers didn't always flow past the areas where goods were needed, and canals were expensive to dig. They were also useless in the winter when the water froze. The advent of railroads made goods transportable anywhere for a reasonable price.

The first effective steam locomotive was the "Rocket," made by John Stephenson in 1829. After his success, a railroad boom erupted across Europe and the United States. The development of the railroad was perhaps most important for the development of the United States because it spans great geographic distances. By 1840 the United States had over 3,000 miles of railroad tracks. The use of railroads created an unprecedented demand for coal to fuel the locomotives and iron to make the tracks. Engineers were needed to build bridges, dig tunnels, and plan routes.

A multitude of companies built and operated the railways. Some were profitable, but most struggled financially. In the beginning, companies were typically formed to build and operate a single railway line between two points. As time passed, however, large railway lines bought out smaller ones. Huge railway companies grew in the process. Cornelius Vanderbuilt, J.P. Morgan, James J. Hill, and Edward Harriman built vast railroad empires in the United States.

Early American railway building was concentrated in the Northeast and industrial Midwest, but it was soon apparent that a transcontinental railway line was needed to connect the east and west coasts. Proposals were made as early as 1845, and many different routes for tracks were discussed and argued over. Construction began in 1864. The Central Pacific line built east from Sacramento, California, and the Union Pacific line built west from Omaha, Nebraska. In 1869 the lines met and were connected at Promontory, Utah, giving the nation coast-to-coast rail service.

Cities with rail traffic experienced economic prosperity. Towns bypassed by the railroads struggled to survive. Railroads were also important for transporting commuters who worked within the city. Industry benefited greatly from reduced transportation costs. Raw materials were brought to the factories at reduced prices, and finished products were easily shipped to their markets.

Though the first railroad building boom occurred from 1830 to 1850, additions and improvements continued. Longer-lasting steel rails replaced rails of iron. Steel bridges replaced those made of wood and iron. Locomotives became more efficient and increased in power. Electric and diesel locomotives eventually replaced those powered by steam. Networks of railroads developed throughout the world and remain one of the most important sources of transportation.

Name_____ Date _____

POINTS TO PONDER

1. Having a railroad depot was important to the prosperity of a town. Why do you think towns with access to railroads fared better than towns without railroad service?

_____

_____

_____

_____

_____

2. The building of railroads benefited a country's economy in dozens of ways. Thousands of jobs were created, and a variety of raw materials and finished products were needed. List some of the jobs created and the products and materials needed to construct and operate a railway line.

_____

_____

_____

_____

_____

3. Today railroads are still important in this country for hauling freight, but they have declined in importance for passenger transportation. As a result, train travel has a romantic appeal for many people. Have you ever traveled by train? If not, would you like to? What appeals to you about train travel?

_____

_____

_____

_____

_____

Name_____ Date_____

CHALLENGES

1. Who produced the first efficient steam engine?

_____

2. What form of transportation first used steam engines?

_____

3. What was the name of the first locomotive?

_____

4. Why did coal and iron production increase due to railroads?

_____

_____

5. Name one of the men who built a railroad empire in the United States.

_____

6. Construction of the transcontinental railroad line started from Sacramento, California, and Omaha, Nebraska. In what state did the two lines meet in 1869?

_____

7. How did other industries benefit from the railroad?

_____

_____

8. Name two improvements in railroads that occurred after 1850.

_____

_____

9. How were most heavy goods transported before the invention of railroads?

_____

10. What problems did this earlier form of transportation have?

_____

_____

_____

COAL AND COAL MINING

Coal was the fuel of the Industrial Revolution. It was used to power the steam engines and locomotives and to heat homes and workshops. Coal and coke (a coal by-product) were an essential part of the steelmaking process, and coal derivatives were important to the chemical industry. Factories tended to build near coal fields in order to guarantee a cheap and easily acquired supply of fuel. In 1800 England used 11 million tons of coal a year. The arrival of the railroads and advances in iron and steelmaking increased demand so that by 1870 England required 100 million tons a year; after that the demand for coal continued to increase.

Coal miners faced dangers such as cave-ins, explosions, and respiratory diseases.

Coal mining has always been a difficult and potentially dangerous job. The technological advances of the Industrial Revolution brought some changes to the mines, but the industry continued to rely heavily on manual labor. Coal miners faced a daunting array of dangers. Cave-ins trapped many miners when tunnels were not sufficiently reinforced. Mines could flood when tunnels were dug under aquifers. Most feared was the threat of underground gases igniting and creating a deadly explosion. Those that survived the immediate dangers of the mines were often stricken with black lung, a respiratory illness caused by years of breathing coal dust. Keeping the mines ventilated was a constant problem.

Carelessness led to many mine accidents. Accidents became more frequent when mine bosses bypassed safety precautions to speed up production. A 1907 survey revealed that 3,197 men were killed in coal mining accidents in the United States that year. The Bureau of Mines was created in 1910 to improve safety regulations as a result of a string of mine accidents.

While coal mining still depended mainly on manual labor, new inventions did improve productivity. Steam engines were introduced to pump water from the mines, allowing tunnels to go deep beneath the water table. Explosives were first used in coal mines in the late 1700s. Their blasting power greatly improved productivity, but explosives remained extremely dangerous for nearly a century. Coal mines in the United States began using "breakers" in the 1830s. Breakers were used at the surface of the mine to sort the coal rocks by size. The coal was dumped in the top of the machine and worked its way through several screens until the different sized rocks were separated.

Unlike factories, coal mines were usually located in rural areas. Many of the miners farmed part-time in addition to working in the coal mines. The operation of a coal mine required a variety of laborers. Miners used dynamite to blow the coal from the walls and to form tunnels. Carpenters and engineers were needed to brace the tunnels. Miner's helpers gathered the coal and filled carts with it. The carts were sometimes pushed by people, but donkeys and ponies were soon used at most mines to pull the carts. Small boys were often employed to lead the donkeys through the mines. Once at the surface, several workers were needed to operate the breakers. Many men worked in the mines all of their lives, spending most of their days underground.

Coal remained the dominant fuel well into the twentieth century. A plentiful and reliable source of coal was a necessity for any country that wanted to achieve industrial self-sufficiency.

Name_____ Date _____

POINTS TO PONDER

1. England, Germany, and the United States had vast coal deposits. Is it likely that the possession of this natural resource is one of the reasons that these countries were among the first to industrialize? Explain.

_____

_____

_____

_____

2. There were a variety of jobs to be performed in a coal mine. Do you think that you would have liked working in a coal mine? Why or why not?

_____

_____

_____

_____

3. Oil has replaced coal as the most important energy source for our economy. Do you think that someday we may develop another energy source that will replace oil? Do you have any ideas about what the new energy source will be?

_____

_____

_____

_____

_____

Name_____ Date_____

CHALLENGES

1. Why did industries tend to locate near coal mines?

_____

_____

2. What two new developments drastically increased the demand for coal?

_____

_____

3. What dangers did coal miners face?

_____

_____

4. Why was the Bureau of Mines created in 1910?

_____

_____

5. What did "breakers" do?

_____

_____

6. What inventions improved productivity in the mines? Did any make mines safer?

_____

_____

7. What were ponies and donkeys used for in the mines?

_____

_____

8. What jobs did young boys perform in the mines?

_____

_____

9. What is "black lung"?

_____

_____

10. Name two common uses for coal.

_____

_____

CHILD LABOR: ABUSES AND REFORMS

Long before the Industrial Revolution, children were expected to work. Under the direction of their parents, young children worked in the fields, in the house, and in cottage industries. By doing this they added to the family income and acquired the skills necessary to support themselves when they got older. Many children, upon reaching the age of 12 or 13, were apprenticed to craftsmen and learned the skills of a blacksmith, carpenter, bricklayer, or some other trade.

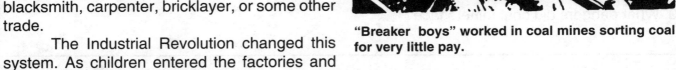

"Breaker boys" worked in coal mines sorting coal for very little pay.

The Industrial Revolution changed this system. As children entered the factories and mines, parental supervision was replaced by the discipline of the foremen, and instead of learning skills through an apprenticeship, children learned only the tedious tasks of operating factory machines.

The demand for unskilled factory workers was high, and child labor met the factories' needs. Children could work for a smaller salary. They were preferred for some jobs in textile mills because their small fingers could better manipulate the cotton threads. In the early days of the factory system, children often worked alongside their parents in the textile mills, because mill owners hired entire families. As the factory evolved, families were routinely broken up, and children worked under the direction of a company overseer. Factory owners often "apprenticed" large numbers of children from orphanages, turning them into virtual slaves who lived only to work at the machines. Impoverished parents were often forced to send their children to work in the factories and mines.

The lives of the child workers were very difficult. Often as young as six years old, they started work as early as five in the morning and worked late into the night. Many of the jobs they performed were dangerous, especially those in coal mines. Their health was poor due to their working conditions and inadequate diet. Foremen often beat them if they worked too slowly. They received no education and learned no skills that gave them hope of employment beyond the factory.

Abolishing the abuses of child labor proved to be difficult. England particularly struggled with the issue. The textile industry used vast numbers of child laborers and was an important part of the English economy. Many political leaders did not believe that it was the job of government to regulate industry. The English Parliament examined child labor in the 1830s and finally passed a number of acts to eliminate the worst abuses over the next decades. The laws limited the working hours and raised the wages of children, as well as prohibited them from performing the most dangerous jobs.

The United States industrialized later than England, but also came to depend on child labor. The 1870 census reported 750,000 workers under the age of 15; that number increased dramatically over the next 30 years. Individual states had passed laws regulating child labor early in the 1800s, but it was clear that national laws were needed. Ministers, doctors, and educators pushed for its abolition. Finally in 1938 the Fair Labor Standards Act prohibited the employment of children under 14 years old and limited the types of jobs that they could perform. This act effectively ended the worst abuses of child labor in the United States.

Name_____ Date_____

POINTS TO CONSIDER

1. Children who spent their time working in factories were unable to receive an education. What long-term effects would there be on a country that used a large portion of its children to perform factory work?

_____

_____

_____

_____

_____

2. In the preindustrial world, children were often apprenticed to a craftsman to learn job skills. This was the most common form of education at the time. By working under the craftsman's instruction, children were trained at an early age to perform a specific job. What advantages do you see in an apprenticeship education? What disadvantages are there? Would such a system work today? Why or why not?

_____

_____

_____

_____

_____

3. Even before the Industrial Revolution children were expected to work hard for the family at an early age. They were also subject to harsh discipline, both at home and at work. Compared to today's standards, life during the Industrial Revolution was quite brutal. What do parents and society require children to do now? Why do you think that attitudes toward children have changed? Do we value children more today?

_____

_____

_____

_____

Name_____ Date_____

CHALLENGES

1. Before the Industrial Revolution, children were often apprenticed to craftsmen. What does an apprentice do?

_____

_____

2. Why did the factory owners hire children?

_____

_____

3. Describe life in the factories or mines for a typical child worker.

_____

_____

4. Why did England find it difficult to abolish child labor?

_____

_____

5. What types of children were usually "apprenticed" by the factory owners?

_____

_____

6. What did English laws regulating child labor try to accomplish?

_____

_____

7. What groups of people led the fight against child labor in the United States?

_____

_____

8. In 1938 America finally passed effective legislation regulating child labor. What was the law called?

_____

_____

WOMEN IN THE INDUSTRIAL REVOLUTION

The textile industry hired many women workers because they could pay women less than men.

The Industrial Revolution transformed women's lives as well as men's. Scholars have long debated whether the Industrial Revolution helped to emancipate women from domination by men, or merely continued their exploitation in different ways. There is no doubt, however, that the rise of factories caused women's work roles to change dramatically.

Before the Industrial Revolution, most people lived in rural areas and farmed the land. Traditionally women worked alongside their husbands in the fields and also did their household chores. Families worked as units for a common income. Women and children worked under the direction of their husbands or fathers.

The Industrial Revolution changed the way in which families earned their livings. Factory work offered women new job possibilities. The 1851 census showed that women made up about 30 percent of England's work force. Many women still worked on the farm or as maids and cooks, but factory work employed two out of five women. Women in factories earned wages independent of their families, and this gave them a new-found freedom. However, women still found themselves under the direction of men, because mill owners and factory supervisors were almost always men. Prevailing attitudes about women's work remained. Women were believed to be mentally and physically incapable of performing certain kinds of work, and they were usually paid less than men.

Because of these prejudices, women were channeled into certain types of work. Half of the workers in textile mills were women, but there were extremely few women who worked in building construction or the steelmaking industry. The textile industry hired women because large numbers of unskilled laborers were needed to produce the fabric. Mill owners preferred to hire women for some jobs. Women could do the work as well as men, but the mill owners could get by with paying them less money. Also, as child labor became less common at the end of the 1800s, women filled more jobs in the textile mills that had previously been done by children.

Even within the textile industry, women were discriminated against. They typically held only the lowest skilled jobs. Positions of responsibility and authority were usually reserved for men. Because women often stopped working after they married, many men felt that there was no reason to train women for skilled jobs since they were normally short-term employees. Other men were simply prejudiced and believed that women were incapable of performing skilled jobs.

Clearly, the Industrial Revolution offered women new opportunities. Yet, due to prevailing attitudes, many of the opportunities open to men were still not open to women, and they had little opportunity to advance beyond the most menial jobs. However, the idea of women earning their own money became acceptable. Opinions regarding women workers gradually changed. In time, women came to be regarded as equally capable and qualified for important and difficult jobs.

Name_____ Date_____

POINTS TO PONDER

1. The Industrial Revolution has been viewed by different writers in different ways. Some believe that the factory was an example of continued control of women by men. Others believe that the opportunity to work away from the family and earn an independent income started women down the road to independence. What is your opinion regarding this matter? Did the Industrial Revolution result only in a new form of exploitation or was it the beginning of women's liberation?

_____

_____

_____

_____

2. Most women who worked in factories worked in the textile industries. Few women worked in iron and steel mills, in construction, or in the mines. Textile mills became a socially acceptable place for women to work, while other jobs were still reserved for men. Today both women and men are usually accepted for all types of work, but some jobs are still dominated by one sex or the other. Can you list some jobs that are usually held by men? How about jobs usually performed by women? Do you think that these distinctions between "women's work" and "men's work" will continue to disappear?

_____

_____

_____

_____

3. Women were almost always paid lower wages than men during the Industrial Revolution. Today national statistics show that women still make less money than men. What do you believe is the reason for this? Do you think that this will change?

_____

_____

_____

_____

Name_____ Date_____

CHALLENGES

1. What types of work did women perform before the Industrial Revolution?

_____

_____

2. How did factory work give women new opportunities?

_____

_____

_____

3. In what industry did most women work?

_____

_____

_____

4. How did laws limiting child labor affect women's job opportunities?

_____

_____

_____

5. Why did factory managers prefer women for some jobs?

_____

_____

_____

6. List two ways that women were discriminated against in the factories.

_____

_____

7. What were the prevailing attitudes during the Industrial Revolution regarding the ability of women to perform skilled work?

_____

_____

_____

8. How did these attitudes change?

_____

_____

_____

LAISSEZ-FAIRE ECONOMICS AND CLASSICAL LIBERALISM

Adam Smith

With the rise of wealthy factory owners, a new class of people was created in England. The upper-middle class of businessmen, industrialists, and bankers became a powerful political force and challenged the power of the large landowners. Their political philosophy is now known as "classical liberalism," and their economic philosophy is called *laissez-faire* ("let it happen") economics.

Laissez-faire economics was a philosophy developed by Adam Smith. In 1776 Smith wrote the book *The Wealth of Nations* in which he criticized the old economic philosophy of "mercantilism" and proposed a new plan for economic growth. Under mercantilism, governments had intervened actively in the economy and had protected their own industries by putting tariffs (taxes) on foreign products coming into the country. Smith proposed that the economy did best when it was left alone by the government (thus the name laissez-faire). He emphasized the importance of trade and of specialization of labor. He harshly attacked the philosophy of mercantilism. Smith believed that the economy operated according to three natural laws. The first was that all persons should follow their own self-interest. The second was that each person was the best judge of his own self-interest. The third was that each person working toward his self-interest would add up to the general welfare of the population.

Smith believed that the natural laws operated best when free from government interference of any type. He believed that business, education, and charity were best left up to individuals. Government should do as little as possible, existing only to provide a military and protect property. David Ricardo expanded upon Smith's ideas by stating that due to the inevitable conflict between businessmen and laborers, workers would always be paid just enough to survive under the natural laws of the economy. Ricardo believed that if workers were paid more, they would have more children and create a surplus of labor that would result in the poverty of all workers. He concluded that workers should not attempt to change their income, because higher wages would only lead to their demise. His theory, the "iron law of wages," held a very bleak forecast for the working class.

The upper-middle classes were quick to embrace the ideas of Smith and Ricardo. Their ideas that government nonintervention was best for the general welfare soothed the consciences of factory owners who got rich while their workers struggled to survive. The ideas of laissez-faire economics became very influential and delayed many badly needed reforms. While the economy grew at a rapid pace and England became a wealthy nation, many suffered in the process. For years the government ignored the problems of child labor, city slums, and an impoverished working class. Public services were nonexistent in most factory cities. Education was neglected, and England gradually fell behind in the discovery and use of new technologies.

While the ideas of laissez-faire economics dominated the minds of local and national leaders, the working classes became more alienated. Convinced that they were being oppressed by the factory owners in league with the government, they turned to more radical ideologies to achieve reform.

POINTS TO PONDER

1. Adam Smith's attitudes toward government intervention were welcomed by the upper classes. Do you believe they were motivated more by greed or by the belief that "natural laws" in the economy destined many workers to live in poverty?

_____

_____

_____

_____

2. England neglected its educational system for decades due to the belief in government non-intervention. Other countries eventually surpassed England's economic achievements. What can we learn from this example? Does the United States need to devote more money and effort to improving its schools?

_____

_____

_____

_____

3. For a century following Adam Smith's book, England experienced unprecedented economic growth. Laissez-faire economics allowed thousands of workers to live in poverty, but also resulted in England becoming the wealthiest and most technologically advanced nation on Earth. Do you think the results justified the costs?

_____

_____

_____

_____

Name_____ Date _____

CHALLENGES

1. What does *laissez-faire* mean?

_____

_____

2. Who was the author of *The Wealth of Nations*?

_____

3. Mercantilism was the dominant economic philosophy before laissez-faire economics. How did governments protect their industries under mercantilism?

_____

_____

4. What did Adam Smith propose that government should do to help the economy?

_____

5. What functions did Smith believe were legitimate roles for government to play?

_____

_____

6. David Ricardo believed that workers would always be impoverished due to natural laws of the economy. What did his set of beliefs regarding worker wages become known as?

_____

7. What types of reforms were delayed due to the belief that government shouldn't interfere?

_____

_____

8. What class of people were most attracted to the laissez-faire economic philosophy?

_____

9. How did the working classes feel about laissez-faire economics?

_____

_____

10. Education was neglected in England due to the belief in government non-intervention. What was the long-term result?

_____

KARL MARX AND THE BIRTH OF SOCIALISM

Karl Marx

Laissez-faire economics caused the gap between the wealthy and poor to widen. As companies grew, workers became more alienated from their employers and came to resent the fact that their labor was enriching factory owners while they, the workers, struggled to survive. National and local governments of the era provided little or no relief. Often the working classes were viewed with distaste and fear by the governing elite. It is not surprising that the working classes viewed laissez-faire economics with suspicion. The values of individualism preached by the wealthy were of small comfort to those born in poverty.

Karl Marx was among those who proposed a different ideology. Marx was not the first socialist or even the best known of his time, but his ideas became the foundation of communist theory in the decades following his death. In 1847 he worked with Friedrich Engels to write *The Communist Manifesto.* In it Marx stated that man lived in a state of nature that forced him to struggle for survival. To succeed in this struggle, men formed relationships with those who had similar interests, resulting in the formation of classes. Marx felt that control of wealth was the most important aspect of a group's position in society. He saw all of history as the story of struggles between different classes for the control of wealth.

The Industrial Revolution had changed the class structure of society. Marx saw two new classes as the most important in the struggle. Marx described the conflicting groups as the bourgeoisie (factory owners and the middle class) and the proletariat (factory workers). Marx was sympathetic toward the proletariat. Marx saw that the changes brought about by the Industrial Revolution had alienated the workers. Rather than having the pride of skilled craftsmen, they performed repetitive, unskilled tasks at their machines. In Marx's opinion, the proletariat were the vibrant, creative class that powered the economy while the bourgeoisie acted as parasites.

Marx believed that conflict between the proletariat and bourgeoisie would grow and that eventually the proletariat would violently overthrow the bourgeoisie. He wrote, "the proletarians have nothing to lose but their chains. They have the world to win. Working men of the world, unite!" After the revolution, he believed that all people would work together toward the common good. All people would contribute their labor, and all would take what they needed. National boundaries would disappear, and different classes would cease to exist because everyone would be equal. These socialist ideas were quite attractive to the working class. Some workers did not accept Marx's ideas of revolution, but they did see the value of banding together to negotiate for better conditions. Others accepted his ideas about a coming revolution and worked toward that goal. Marx became recognized as the philosophical father of communism.

Communist revolutions took place in several countries. Russia, China, Vietnam, and several other nations have had communist governments in the twentieth century, but the world revolution and classless society that Marx envisioned has not occurred. With its failure in Russia, it would appear that communism's days as a viable philosophy have ended.

Name_____ Date _____

POINTS TO PONDER

1. Marx felt that the struggle for wealth was the primary motivation of all men. Do you agree with this analysis, or are there other things that motivate people? List other things that motivate us that Marx may have underestimated.

_____

_____

_____

_____

_____

2. Marx's ideas were attractive to many members of the working class. Why do you think that workers were attracted to his ideas? Compare Marx's beliefs with those of the laissez-faire economists. Do Marx's ideas give workers more hope?

_____

_____

_____

_____

3. Marx envisioned a classless society after the revolution. Communist revolutions occurred in several countries, but economic equality was never obtained. Rather than working for the common good of all, most workers became frustrated and disillusioned in communist countries. Was Marx's goal unrealistic? Does human nature demand that we be directly rewarded for our work?

_____

_____

_____

_____

_____

Name_____ Date_____

CHALLENGES

1. Why were the working classes dissatisfied with the prevailing economic system?

_____

_____

2. How did individuals in power tend to view the working class during Marx's time?

_____

_____

3. What was the name of the book that Marx wrote with Friedrich Engels?

_____

4. What did Marx believe man's basic struggle throughout history was?

_____

_____

5. What two groups were defined by Marx as the bourgeoisie and proletariat?

_____

_____

6. Which side was Marx sympathetic toward?

_____

7. How did Marx predict that the conflict between proletariat and bourgeoisie would end?

_____

_____

8. Name a country that experienced a communist revolution.

_____

9. What did Marx predict would happen to the different classes of people after the revolution?

_____

_____

10. Were Marx's predictions regarding the revolution accurate?

_____

ATTEMPTS AT REFORM: ALTERNATE VISIONS

Karl Marx was not the only man to propose ideas for reform. Other men had different proposals for a more humane society. Among the early reformers was an English industrialist named Robert Owen.

Robert Owen was a wealthy factory owner, but he was quite concerned with the plight of his employees. He desired to provide a better working and living environment for his workers and their families. To test his vision Owen built a model factory and community in New Lanarck, Scotland. He provided good housing and schools for the

George Pullman's railroad car factory

children and paid his workers higher wages. His competitors were astounded to find that he was able to do this and still have a profitable company. The improved living conditions had resulted in higher worker productivity. In 1824 Owen attempted a more radical plan in New Harmony, Indiana. New Harmony was a voluntary socialist community where each member worked for the good of the group and the group provided equal care for all members. New Harmony was a failure, however, because the members were unable to cooperate effectively. Though Owen never established another society, men such as Charles Fourier, William Thompson, and Claude de Saint-Simon were influenced by his social experiments and attempted similar versions of Owen's model societies.

An alternate vision for reform was attempted by George Pullman. Like Owen, Pullman was a wealthy industrialist. He had made his fortune building railroad passenger cars famous for their comfort. Pullman believed that city life was the cause of poor job performance and worker discontent. He proposed to build a company-owned town that would avoid the vices of the city. In 1880 Pullman bought seven square miles of property south of Chicago and built the town of Pullman. The new town was well planned compared to other cities. All of its streets were paved, and it had numerous parks, good schools, well-constructed housing, and excellent sanitation. Athletic events, a theater, and a large library were provided to entertain the population. Alcohol, prostitution, and other vices commonly associated with large cities were strictly forbidden. Pullman ruled the town harshly. His opinion was the only one that counted in political matters, but for the first few years the company town was a success.

Pullman's problems began when an economic depression occurred in 1893. Though his company was still very profitable, he worried about future sales. Pullman elected to cut costs by firing many of his workers and reducing pay for those that remained. He kept the rent on the workers' houses at the same high rates, however, and this put them in an impossible situation. Unions had never been allowed in Pullman's factories, but at this point the workers felt that they had nothing to lose. They allied themselves with Eugene Debs and the American Railroad Union and began a strike that lasted for several weeks. Eventually the strike was broken by federal troops, and some of the workers returned to work, but the concept of Pullman's company town was proved a failure in the process. Pullman had hoped to pacify his workers by providing them with a pleasant place to live. He found, however, that if they were not paid a fair wage they would not be content.

Name_____ Date_____

POINTS TO PONDER

1. Robert Owen's factory at New Lanarck provided better living and working conditions for his workers. His competitors didn't believe that he would be able to make his factory profitable, but Owen's workers were more productive in his model community. Why do you think this happened?

_____

_____

_____

_____

_____

2. Like Owen, George Pullman also provided a pleasant living environment for his workers. However, when wages were reduced, the workers became very dissatisfied. Are wage levels more important than living conditions?

_____

_____

_____

_____

_____

3. George Pullman provided a peaceful, well-managed community for his workers to live and work in. However, the people of the town gave up some personal freedoms in the process. Would you be willing to give up some freedoms to live in the type of model community that Pullman created?

_____

_____

_____

_____

33

Name_____ Date _____

CHALLENGES

1. Where did Robert Owen build his first model community?

_____

2. How was it different from most factory towns?

_____

_____

3. New Harmony, Indiana, was Robert Owen's second experimental community. Why did it fail?

_____

_____

4. What product did George Pullman produce in his factories?

_____

5. List some of the advantages that the town of Pullman offered its residents.

_____

_____

6. What types of things were banned from the town of Pullman?

_____

_____

7. What was the cause of the worker rebellion in Pullman in 1893?

_____

_____

8. The workers at Pullman allied themselves with the American Railway Union and went on strike. How did the strike end?

_____

_____

9. Pullman's vision for his company town ended in failure. What assumption did he make that caused this failure?

_____

_____

THE GROWTH OF LABOR UNIONS

The nineteenth century was the era of big business. Powerful men such as Andrew Carnegie and J.P. Morgan ruthlessly pursued greater and greater profits. Yet this was also the time period when labor unions first became a powerful force in American life. Individual workers were almost powerless to change their status, but when they banded together to form unions, the workers found that they could effectively bargain for better wages, shorter hours, and safer working conditions.

Workers organized into unions often used the strike as a bargaining tool.

Labor unions were not an American idea. Unions had existed in Europe long before they gained strength in America. Yet American unions were unique in their nature. European unions tended to base much of their philosophy on the ideas of Karl Marx and tended to view strikes by workers as the beginning of revolution. American labor unions had different ideas. Most American unions did not want to create a revolution but merely wanted better wages and working conditions. The first American unions were local organizations, formed in the late 1700s. These unions were organized by workers in skilled crafts but never were influential beyond the cities where they were located. The first successful national union was the Knights of Labor, formed in Philadelphia in 1869. The Knights welcomed all types of workers in their union and by 1886 had 700,000 members. Disagreements among union leaders caused the Knights of Labor to disintegrate. More successful was the American Federation of Labor (AFL). The AFL was led by Samuel Gompers and was exclusively for skilled industrial workers. Gompers organized the AFL as a loose confederation. Local trade unions were allowed to form their own rules and negotiate their own contracts, but the local union chapters were also part of the AFL. By 1904 the AFL had 1.6 million members. It had become the dominant national union in America.

Industrial leaders did not welcome the unions. Many industrialists forbade their workers to join unions and fired workers who tried to organize them. The industrialists knew that the workers were powerful negotiators when they were organized and did not want to have their profits reduced by being forced to pay union workers higher wages or by being forced to shut down their factories while workers were on strike. The American government also viewed the unions with suspicion. Government tended to side with the factory owners in disputes between workers and management. Both sides could be blamed for strike violence, however. Strikes at Homestead (1892) and Pullman (1893) both ended in violence and the defeat of the unions. Yet these strikes and others like them also strengthened the will of union members and made management leaders appear greedy and heartless.

The unions were the great reformers of the era. The lack of government regulation in industry resulted in horrible working conditions. Shorter work weeks and safer working conditions were often at the heart of union negotiations. Eventually unions were accepted as legitimate organizations by the government, although union goals were still opposed by many politicians. In 1933 the National Labor Relations Act guaranteed unions the right to organize, affirming the place that unions have in industry.

Name_____ Date _____

POINTS TO PONDER

1. What reasons would workers have to want to form unions? Are there also reasons why workers might prefer not to join unions? What are they?

_____

_____

_____

_____

_____

2. Initially, national and local governments in the United States tended to view unions with suspicion and even opposition. Why do you think that government was opposed to unions in the late 1800s? Remember the character of European unions and the role big business had in the government.

_____

_____

_____

_____

_____

3. The initial goals of most American unions were increasing worker wages and improving working conditions. Today wages are much higher than when unions started, and the government regulates factory conditions to ensure safety. Are labor unions still necessary, or have they achieved their goals and become obsolete?

_____

_____

_____

_____

_____

Name_____ Date_____

CHALLENGES

1. What did labor unions give workers the ability to do?

_____

_____

2. How were European unions different from American unions regarding their views on revolution?

_____

_____

3. What were the primary goals of most American labor unions?

_____

_____

_____

4. What was the name of the first national American labor union?

_____

5. Who was the leader of the American Federation of Labor (AFL)?

_____

6. How did most industrialists and businessmen view the new unions?

_____

_____

_____

7. Name one of the large national strikes of the 1890s that turned violent.

_____

8. What did the National Labor Relations Act of 1933 guarantee?

_____

_____

9. The AFL gave its members a large degree of local control. What activities did the local trade unions control?

_____

_____

10. How did the American government initially view the labor unions? How did its opinion change?

_____

_____

IMPERIALISM AND THE INDUSTRIAL REVOLUTION

In the early 1870s Europe began its great Imperial Age. Large sections of Asia and Africa were either conquered or claimed as colonies by the industrialized nations. The colonies were either ruled directly by their conquerors or indirectly through native rulers who were controlled by the Europeans. England, France, Belgium, Germany, and the Netherlands became the rulers of vast areas of the globe, while other European nations held smaller colonies.

European countries controlled colonies in Asia and Africa that supplied raw materials and new markets for European goods.

The Industrial Revolution contributed directly to the European nations' abilities to rule over their colonies. Europe's industrial strength gave its armies weapons that were vastly superior to anything that the Asian and African societies could produce. For example, an army of only 75,000 British troops was able to control the millions of people of India. The advent of the steamship also gave Europeans the ability to easily cross oceans and made ruling distant colonies more practical.

The countries of Europe had many reasons for conquering distant colonial people. Some justified holding colonies as a means to spread Christianity. Control of colonial areas allowed missionaries to preach unrestricted by local laws. Others believed colonies were a source of national pride for the ruling nation. Competition between the various nations for control of Africa and Asia was certainly fierce, and relations between European nations often became strained as a result. Some believed that they had a duty to "civilize" the conquered peoples, ignoring the fact that native peoples already had civilizations that had existed for centuries. In their arrogance, Europeans believed that their own civilization was the best and that all people should imitate it. Economy also played a major role in the building of colonies. Europeans had become dependent on many items that were not available in their home countries. Coffee and tea had become staples of the European diet. Rubber, petroleum, cotton, copper, and a variety of other raw materials were needed for European industries. A steady supply of these raw materials was vital to the European economies. The European countries took over the productive life of the colonies so that their own industries could prosper.

The colonies also provided a source for European investments and products. The colonial territories had not yet begun to industrialize, and thus needed railroads, mines, warehouses, docks, factories, and refineries. European investors provided these structures, often at a handsome profit. Free trade between the colony and ruling country also brought new markets to suppliers. European products were readily purchased by the native populations, but often bankrupted local producers who could not compete using preindustrial methods.

Essentially, the colonies were exploited by Europeans. In some cases the native populations were treated quite cruelly by their conquerors. In almost all cases, the colonized people resented their European rulers. After World War I, pressure mounted on the nations to free their colonies. Sporadic revolts broke out, and one by one the colonies freed themselves from European rule. By the 1960s most of the colonies had become free and independent nations.

Name_____ Date _____

POINTS TO PONDER

1. European leaders cited a variety of reasons for holding colonies. List them. Do any of the reasons seem justifiable to you?

_____

_____

_____

_____

_____

2. During the nineteenth century European societies possessed vastly superior technical knowledge compared to African and Asian societies. Is it surprising that Europeans were tempted to conquer these less developed societies? Does their technological superiority justify their belief that European culture was superior and that they had a "civilizing mission"?

_____

_____

_____

_____

_____

3. The native population of the colonies generally came to resent their European rulers, and occasionally, open rebellion broke out. Why do you think that the native people felt this way toward the Europeans?

_____

_____

_____

_____

_____

Name_____ Date_____

CHALLENGES

1. In what decade did Europe begin its great Imperial Age?

_____

2. On what two continents were most of Europe's colonies located?

_____

3. How did the Industrial Revolution contribute to Europe's ability to conquer new colonies?

_____

_____

4. What reasons did Europeans give to justify conquering their colonies?

_____

_____

5. What types of raw materials did the European countries import from their colonies?

_____

_____

6. What contributions did Europeans make to the colonial economies?

_____

_____

7. How did most of the native people of the colonies feel about their European rulers?

_____

_____

8. When did pressure begin to mount for Europeans to free their colonies?

_____

_____

9. Name three European countries that ruled colonial empires.

_____

10. When did the last colonies free themselves from European rule?

_____

THE AGE OF IRON AND STEEL

Pittsburgh became one of the steel-making centers of the United States.

Though the art of iron production was mastered many centuries before the Industrial Revolution, iron was extremely expensive and was only used in small quantities where cheaper materials could not be substituted. Before the Industrial Revolution iron products were produced in small forges by a time-consuming process. Primitive blast-furnaces produced pig iron, but it was unusable because it was too brittle due to its high carbon content. Blacksmiths refined the iron by hand. By alternately heating and hammering it, carbon was removed and the iron ultimately achieved its desired strength and shape. The process required skill, strength, and a great deal of patience.

A sequence of new techniques made iron easier to produce. The process of puddling and rolling was introduced in England in 1781. By this technique iron ore was added to the pig iron in the furnace. This caused a chemical reaction that separated the carbon and allowed the operator to remove the molten iron. The puddled iron was then rolled between steel rollers into a bar of iron that was suitable for railway lines or chain links.

Steelmaking also benefited from improved techniques. Steel is a variety of iron with a carbon content of .5 to 1.5 percent. Steel was superior to puddled iron because it was stronger and more durable. It was also far more expensive because it couldn't be made in large quantities. There was no known way to remove more of the carbon and other impurities from large amounts of the metal.

Two solutions to this problem were discovered in the 1850s. The first technique was developed in 1856 by the English gentleman Sir Henry Bessemer. The "Bessemer process" used a converter to blow hot air through molten pig iron. This caused the impurities in the pig iron to oxidize, creating steel. In 1858 Pierre Martin and Werner Siemens introduced a new type of furnace for steel production. Their open hearth furnace resembled the furnaces used for puddling iron but burned incandescent gases to achieve a much higher temperature. The higher temperatures kept the metal liquefied and allowed impurities to be removed and steel to be produced. These new techniques allowed steel prices to drop dramatically. Steel replaced iron in railroads, tools, and weapons. England took the lead in the production of steel for awhile, but by the 1880s the United States surpassed England in both the volume of steel produced and in the use of new technologies in the steel industry. By 1918 American companies were producing 45 million tons of steel a year, compared to 9 million tons in England and 14 million tons in Germany.

Midwestern American cities such as Pittsburgh, Chicago, Gary, Youngstown, and Cleveland became the centers of steel manufacture and were dominated by large steel companies. The Mesabi iron ore range near Duluth, Minnesota, became the sight of extensive mining efforts that provided iron ore for the steel industry. Coal mines in Pennsylvania, Kentucky, and West Virginia produced the coal to fuel the furnaces. Railroads were built to transport the coal, and freighters shipped iron ore across the Great Lakes to the centers of steel production. The United States exported large amounts of the steel that it produced and became a wealthy nation.

Name_____ Date_____

POINTS TO PONDER

1. Imagine living in the time before the Industrial Revolution, when iron and steel were rare and expensive. Think of items that we take for granted that would have been unavailable. List several.

_____

_____

_____

_____

2. Steel was often referred to as the "driving force of the American economy." In your opinion, what did that mean? Think of all of the raw materials that go into steel, and all of the finished products that are made from it. What other industries benefited from the steel industry?

_____

_____

_____

_____

3. The Bessemer process and the open hearth furnace made the production of steel less expensive. Prices for steel and steel products declined drastically as a result. When new technology was introduced in the textile industry, fabric prices dropped. New technology still lowers prices today. Though these new technologies bring the benefits of increased production and lower prices, the people and communities who work with the old technologies are left behind, losing jobs and lifestyles. How then, do you feel about "progress" in our world? Do the benefits received by the majority outweigh the misfortune of the few left behind? Should those communities and people left behind be compensated, or left to endure on their own?

_____

_____

_____

_____

Name_____ Date_____

CHALLENGES

1. Why was iron rarely used in large quantities before the Industrial Revolution?

_____

_____

2. Early blacksmiths had to refine pig iron to make it usable. How did they do this?

_____

_____

3. Why was steel superior to iron?

_____

_____

4. How did the Bessemer process work?

_____

_____

5. What was the name of the furnace invented by Pierre Martin and Werner Siemens?

_____

6. Name three of the leading steel-producing cities mentioned.

_____

_____

7. Where is the Mesabi iron ore range located?

_____

_____

8. Name two of the leading states that provided coal for the steel industry.

_____

9. What role did improved transportation techniques play in the United States steel industry?

_____

_____

CARNEGIE, MORGAN, AND THE AMERICAN STEEL INDUSTRY

J. P. Morgan

Andrew Carnegie was an American success story. As a child he worked in a cotton mill for $1.20 a week. Young Carnegie soon began making remarkably successful investments. On different occasions he was involved in bridge building, oil companies, and iron production. He achieved his greatest power and wealth in steel production.

Carnegie led the consolidation movement in steel production. He formed Carnegie Steel Company in 1892. In it he brought together plants from several different cities, basing his operations in Pittsburgh. Carnegie was successful for several reasons. He constantly strove to increase production levels in his plants. He desired to produce the highest quality product for the lowest possible cost. To do this he hired the best chemists and metallurgists. He was an aggressive salesman who was ruthless when dealing with competitors. Both legal and illegal actions were taken to drive his competitors out of business. Carnegie also became involved in many industries related to steel production. This type of involvement was known as "vertical integration." He purchased mines to provide his plants with coal and iron ore, and railroads and steamships to transfer the coal and ore to his factories. Carnegie was the first to practice vertical integration on a large scale, and his pattern is a model that has been copied by countless companies.

By 1901 Carnegie was an old man who had tired of the steel industry. He sold Carnegie Steel to J.P. Morgan, a wealthy banker and railroad man, for $492 million, an enormous sum at the time. Freed of the responsibilities of running his company, he devoted the rest of his life to giving away his fortune. Carnegie once said, "The man who dies rich, dies disgraced," and thousands of libraries, hospitals, and colleges received money from Carnegie to finance new buildings.

While Carnegie distributed his fortune, J.P. Morgan continued the expansion of his steel empire. Shortly after purchasing the company, Morgan refashioned it into the enormous U.S. Steel Corporation. Morgan continued the process of vertically integrating the company. By controlling the raw materials and transportation needed for steel production, Morgan was able to operate U.S. Steel without worrying about outside interference. At the formation of the company, U.S. Steel controlled 60 percent of the steel production in America. It produced half of America's rails and nearly all of its wire and nails.

Pittsburgh was the most important of the steel producing cities for nearly a century. It possessed many of the ingredients necessary for a successful steel industry. It was near large coal and limestone deposits, had a navigable river to provide transportation, and had a large enough business community to provide investors and aggressive businessmen. It lacked iron ore, but this was easily transported by freighters across the Great Lakes from Minnesota.

Men such as Carnegie and Morgan dominated the end of the nineteenth century. They piled up riches in an age before income taxes, government regulations, or strong unions. In the last decades of the nineteenth century, big business dominated American life and politics like it never had before and never has since.

Name_____ Date _____

POINTS TO CONSIDER

1. Andrew Carnegie spent the last years of his life giving away the wealth that he had accumulated. Some people say it was because he was a generous man. Others believe that he wanted to change his image from that of a ruthless businessman to that of a generous person. Some thought he had a guilty conscience for living in wealth while his workers struggled. What reason do you think Carnegie had for giving away so much money?

_____

_____

_____

_____

_____

2. Big business was extremely powerful at the end of the nineteenth century. The government essentially allowed businessmen to do whatever they wanted to do. There was no income tax and very little government regulation. Was this a good situation for American business? Was it good for the American people? As there were no government regulations, do you think that the businessmen were more likely to abuse their power than they are today?

_____

_____

_____

_____

3. The steel industry was one of the most important sectors of the American economy for several decades. In recent years it has diminished in importance and has in fact struggled to compete with the steel industries of other countries. What industries do you think are now important in the United States? What types of companies do you think will be more important in the future?

_____

_____

_____

_____

_____

Name_____ Date_____

CHALLENGES

1. Where did Andrew Carnegie work as a child?

_____

2. What city was the base of Carnegie Steel?

_____

3. What strategies did Carnegie employ that made him a successful businessman?

_____

_____

4. Carnegie was among the first to make his company "vertically integrated." What does this mean?

_____

_____

5. What did Carnegie do with his money after he sold Carnegie Steel to J.P. Morgan?

_____

_____

6. What name did J.P. Morgan give his new company?

_____

7. Why was Pittsburgh a good location for the steel industry?

_____

_____

8. What percentage of steel production did U.S. Steel control?

_____

9. Few limitations were placed on businessmen in the nineteenth century. List two modern factors that Carnegie and Morgan didn't have to face.

_____

_____

10. What did Carnegie think about men who died wealthy?

_____

_____

THE CHEMICAL REVOLUTION

Early chemists had a limited knowledge of their field and usually made their discoveries through trial and error. However, chemists soon learned much about the chemical world and had begun to be more systematic in their experimentation than inventors in other fields.

Chemists were important for their ability to synthetically produce substances that either do not exist naturally, or exist only in small quantities. Many of these synthetic substances are better suited to certain tasks than natural products. The chemical industry did not employ large numbers of workers, nor were its discoveries always noticeable in people's daily lives. Yet advances and innovations in chemistry had drastic effects on industry and brought many improvements to the world.

Chemical advances contributed to a variety of industries. England was the leading developer of chemical technology, as it was of many areas of industry. Alkalies such as sulfuric acid and chlorine bleaches were vital to the textile industry. Synthetic production of alkalies was first developed by Nicholas Leblanc in the 1780s, and the Leblanc process was widely used in England. England's early dominance in chemical production and development soon ended, however. England's educational system was very poor and resulted in few trained scientists and inadequate research facilities. The poor educational system affected England's ability to compete in the production and development of new chemicals even more than it affected its other industries.

Germany overtook England and became the dominant chemical producing country. Its superior public education system produced the scientists necessary to succeed in chemistry. Germany especially came to dominate the production and development of synthetic dyes. A variety of colorful, synthetic dyes were developed from coal tar in the 1870s. These dyes were especially important to the textile industry, the most important industry in England. Due to its inability to compete with the Germans in dye production and development, England was forced to import nearly all of the dyes needed by its textile industry.

A variety of other chemical discoveries had lasting effects, and important discoveries occurred at a rapid pace in the late 1800s. Throughout the late nineteenth century advances in metal alloy research allowed chemists to engineer ways to make different types of steel. Methods for producing paper from wood pulp were developed in the 1850s, making paper much more plentiful and affordable. Alfred Nobel invented nitroglycerine in 1863 and dynamite in 1866. The first synthetic clothing material, later named rayon, was produced as a substitute for silk. In 1886 aluminum, a light, yet strong, metal, was first produced by using the Hall-Heroult process. George Eastman combined new chemical discoveries to improve photography and developed the first handheld camera in 1888. Synthetic ammonia was produced and widely used in agricultural fertilizers, resulting in more abundant food supplies. In 1909 the first plastic (Bakelite) was produced by Leo Baekeland. Plastics soon replaced other materials in a wide variety of uses.

These inventions and many others provided lasting benefits to mankind. Continued improvements were made in chemical fields, and chemistry remained important to industry, agriculture, and medicine.

Name_____ Date_____

POINTS TO PONDER

1. A poor educational system was part of the reason that England lost its early lead in chemical development. Is it important that we stress science education to keep up with other nations in industrial development?

_____

_____

_____

_____

_____

2. The first plastic was produced by Leo Baekeland in 1909. Plastic now is used in numerous items. List several.

_____

_____

_____

_____

_____

3. Chemistry continues to be important in our world today. Can you think of any recent developments that have improved our lives?

_____

_____

_____

_____

_____

_____

Name_____ Date_____

CHALLENGES

1. What important types of substances did chemists develop?

_____

_____

2. What country was the early leader in developing chemical technology?

_____

3. What country later became the dominant chemical producer?

_____

4. What advantage did that country have that greatly assisted the chemical industry?

_____

_____

5. A variety of synthetic dyes were developed in the 1870s from what material?

_____

6. What was the name for the first synthetic clothing material?

_____

7. Alfred Nobel developed two types of explosives. What were they?

_____

8. What synthetic product did Leo Baekeland produce in 1909?

_____

9. Nicholas Leblanc was among the first important chemists. What substance did the Leblanc process produce?

_____

10. What industry benefited directly from Leblanc's discovery?

_____

11. What method helped make paper more plentiful and affordable?

_____

12. The use of what substance resulted in increased food supplies?

_____

ELECTRICITY

Perhaps the greatest advance in the last decades of the nineteenth century was the harnessing of electric power. Electricity provided a new power source for lighting, transport, and home appliances. Few inventions have done more to improve our lives than the electric generator and light bulb. From 1830 to 1890 the railroads were the dominant force in the American economy. For the next 40 years, however, it was the production of electricity and electric appliances and equipment that drove the economy.

The first electric generator was invented in 1831 by Michael Faraday in England. Later inventors improved on his design but retained the principles of the first generator. Electricity's uses were limited, however, until Thomas Edison developed the first serviceable light bulb in 1880.

Henry Ford, Herbert Hoover, and Thomas Edison inspect a recreation of Edison's Menlo Park laboratory.

Edison had set up an "inventor's laboratory" in Menlo Park, New Jersey. Edison had already developed the first phonograph here before working on the light bulb. The problem presented by the light bulb was to find a filament to place inside the bulb that would not burn out quickly. Edison tried hundreds of different materials, finally settling on a type of bamboo that would burn for about 40 hours. Edison also became involved in constructing power generators and constructed the first central power station in 1882 to electrify New York City. Edison formed the General Electric Company to produce lamps and to run the power stations across the country. At first providing electricity far from the power plant presented a problem. George Westinghouse developed alternating current transformers and motors to solve this problem. Alternating current was far more efficient, and despite Edison's opposition it became the standard for the industry.

Electric lighting was an immediate success. Previously, cities had employed less efficient gas lights to brighten their streets, while homes had used gas lamps and candles. The appearance of the cities changed rapidly, and electric wires soon crisscrossed streets and alleys. Electric signs were soon used for advertising, and electric lights were of immense benefit to theaters. Industry was quick to adopt the use of electricity, both for lighting and to run electrically powered machinery. Large companies were formed to provide electricity and produce new markets for industry.

Transportation was greatly enhanced by electricity. Horse drawn carriages and trolleys had been the primary forms of transportation within cities. Electric trolleys provided a much better form of mass transportation. Similar technology was used to power the first subways and electric trains. The electric trolleys allowed city dwellers to travel longer distances across the city more easily, and trolley lines to the city outskirts led to the development of suburbs. Workers were able to more easily commute to their jobs while living outside the center of the city.

American homes lagged behind industry and transportation in early electricity use. In 1907, only 8 percent of all homes had electricity, but this figure rapidly grew to 35 percent by 1920 and 68 percent by 1930. Nearly all city homes had electricity by this point, but rural areas remained without electricity. In 1935 President Franklin Roosevelt created the Rural Electrification Administration to bring electricity to rural areas, thus completing the electrification of America.

Name_____ Date_____

POINTS TO PONDER

1. Imagine a home without electricity. What appliances and devices would you miss most?

_____

_____

_____

_____

_____

2. Publicly owned electric trolleys were eventually replaced by privately owned automobiles as the major form of transportation. Why do you think that most people preferred to drive automobiles rather than ride a trolley?

_____

_____

_____

_____

_____

3. Thomas Edison was the primary developer of electric power and America's most famous inventor. In addition to the light bulb, Edison created versions of the phonograph, motion picture projector and camera, and an improved version of the telephone. What type of skills do you think it takes to be an inventor? What personality traits would be necessary to succeed?

_____

_____

_____

_____

_____

Name_____ Date_____

CHALLENGES

1. Who invented the first electric generator?

_____

2. What was the primary problem that Edison faced in inventing the light bulb?

_____

_____

3. In what city did Edison construct the first central power station?

_____

4. What company did Edison form to produce electrical appliances and to operate the power stations across the country?

_____

5. What invention did George Westinghouse produce that increased the efficiency of the electric generators?

_____

6. What new forms of transportation were developed that used electric power?

_____

_____

7. How did the appearance of cities change after electricity became available?

_____

_____

8. In 1935 President Franklin Roosevelt created the Rural Electrification Administration. What did this agency do?

_____

_____

9. What types of lighting had been employed before the electric light bulb?

_____

10. How did electric trolleys change the locations where workers lived?

_____

_____

HENRY FORD AND THE MODEL T

Ford's Highland Park, Michigan, Model T assembly line

For decades men had dreamed of a horseless carriage. Attempts were made to develop a carriage powered by the same heavy steam engines that propelled locomotives, but the vehicles were not practical. In 1860 Joseph Lenoir invented the first internal combustion engine. Using the same principles as today's automobile engines, Lenoir's internal combustion engine ran on gas. It was much smaller and lighter than the commonly used steam engine and provided a new power source for a practical automobile. By 1890 several men had designed automobiles, but cars still weren't practical for public use.

Among the early designers was Henry Ford. Ford had worked at a variety of jobs, usually as a designer or manufacturer of machines. Like many tinkerers of the time, he soon became interested in the idea of producing an automobile. Ford built his first car in 1893. Interested in building automobiles full time, he formed the Ford Motor Company in 1903. Though automobiles were becoming more common, they were still a luxury item. They were notoriously undependable because the manufacturers were still experimenting with new designs and models.

While most automobile companies were building expensive cars, Henry Ford wanted to build a car that was more affordable. At the same time he demanded that his cars be of the highest quality. Based in Detroit, the Ford Motor Company produced a variety of models, starting with the Model A in 1903. Ford achieved his greatest success with the Model T, and produced it from 1908 to 1927. The Model T was easily the best-constructed and most popular car of its time. The Model T was built with standardized parts and was made of Vanadium steel, the strongest steel available. The standardized parts assured that each Model T was of identical quality and that replacement parts could be easily purchased. It ran reliably and could navigate the rough and muddy roads of the era. Ford sold 10,000 Model Ts at a price of $825 each in the model's first year of production. Henry Ford liked to joke that the Model T was available in "any color—so long as it's black."

Ford soon found that he was unable to keep up with demand. Automakers had always had a single work group build cars from start to finish. Ford was the first to devise an automobile assembly line. In it, each worker performed one simple task on the car. As the assembly line moved forward, the vehicle slowly took shape until it became a completed automobile. This process allowed Ford to construct cars quickly and cheaply. It also allowed Ford to use unskilled workers for many jobs instead of skilled technicians. The jobs were monotonous, but Ford paid the workers well. He instituted a five-dollar-a-day minimum wage, a generous salary for the time.

By 1914 Ford's Model T accounted for half of all cars sold in America. By the time Ford stopped production of the Model T in 1927, 15 million had been sold. The car brought dramatic changes to America. For the first time, a wide range of Americans was able to afford an automobile, and cars soon became a central part of American life. Eventually the dominance of the Ford Motor Company faded, but Henry Ford's ideas for assembly line production and his belief in building an affordable car continued to influence automakers around the world.

Name_____ Date_____

POINTS TO PONDER

1. What qualities did the Model T possess that made it a successful and popular car? Do we look for the same qualities in cars today?

_____

_____

_____

_____

_____

2. Assembly line jobs are quite dull and repetitive, but often pay well. Would you be willing to take a boring job for a large salary, or is it important that you enjoy your work?

_____

_____

_____

_____

_____

3. Imagine life before automobiles were available. How do you think people's lives were changed when they were able to purchase their first car?

_____

_____

_____

_____

_____

_____

_____

Name_____ Date_____

CHALLENGES

1. What invention did Joseph Lenoir contribute to the automobile?

_____

2. What company did Henry Ford found in 1903?

_____

3. Henry Ford desired to build cars that were of high_____ and low_____.

4. What was the name of the first car that Henry Ford's company produced?

_____

5. What was the name of Henry Ford's most successful car?

_____

6. What production method did Ford devise to replace the work group method for building automobiles?

_____

7. How much did Ford pay as a daily minimum wage?

_____

8. How many Model T's had Ford sold by the time production stopped in 1927?

_____

9. How did the low price of Ford's cars change the lives of Americans?

_____

_____

10. Ford's early cars were only available in one color. What was it?

_____

11. Ford used standardized parts in his cars. What were the advantages of standardized parts?

_____

_____

_____

THE WRIGHT BROTHERS

For centuries men had gazed up at the sky and wished that they could join the birds in flight. Hundreds of men had wrestled with the question of how man could free himself from gravity and take to the air. Greek mythology spoke of the inventor Daedalus who constructed wings of bird feathers to achieve flight. Early inventors attempted similar devices, designing wings that men were to wear and flap to achieve flight. All of their attempts failed, often with disastrous consequences for the person attempting to use the wings.

The Wright brothers' first successful flight occurred December 17, 1903.

Lack of success did not deter more inventors from trying to achieve flight. A degree of success was achieved in 1783 when the Montgolfier brothers succeeded in designing the first hot air balloon. While the hot air balloon was a remarkable discovery, it did not provide a practical means of transportation because of its lack of steering.

Progress was made in achieving flight when men abandoned the idea of imitating the flapping motion used by birds. Inventors such as Octave Chanute, Otto Lilienthal, and Percy Pilcher designed and flew the first gliders in the late 1800s. The gliders were light, fragile, unpowered structures that were able to glide through the air for several seconds when taking off from the top of a hill. Rather than flapping, the wings on these gliders were fixed in place. These early gliders provided the foundation for future developments in powered flight.

The brothers Orville and Wilbur Wright were interested in flight at an early age. They learned all that they could about the activities of aviation pioneers and soon began performing their own experiments at their bicycle shop in Dayton, Ohio. Adopting many of the designs and methods of other inventors along with ideas of their own, the Wright brothers built a glider and selected Kitty Hawk, North Carolina, as the place to conduct their experiments.

From 1900 to 1902 the Wright brothers made several trips to Kitty Hawk to test their gliders. From their short flights on the gliders, they developed an effective steering mechanism and learned how to keep the glider on a steady course. There were several accidents during the learning process, and the gliders were often damaged and repaired. With each flight the Wright brothers learned more, and they soon gained the confidence to move beyond gliders and attempt to build and fly the first airplane.

The Wright brothers faced many challenges in designing the plane. They were able to use the frame of their glider but had to design propellers and a light, yet powerful, engine. The plane built by the Wright brothers looks different than those built today. The tail, called the "elevator" by the brothers, was located in the front. The propellers faced the rear of the plane. The pilot rode on the middle of the wing rather than inside a cockpit.

The Wright brothers returned to Kitty Hawk, and the plane made its first successful flight on December 17, 1903, with Orville at the controls. The first flight lasted less than a minute, but as the brothers gained experience at the controls, longer flights were made. Over the next years, the brothers continued to work on improved aircraft designs, and airplanes came to resemble the styles we are familiar with today. The Wright brothers' first plane was primitive, but marked the beginning of a revolutionary new form of transportation.

Name_____ Date_____

POINTS TO PONDER

1. Several generations of aviation pioneers were convinced that flapping wings were the key to achieving flight. Numerous failures did not prevent further attempts. Why do you think that the early inventors were obsessed with flapping wings?

_____

_____

_____

_____

_____

2. Many of the aviation pioneers were killed or seriously injured in their experiments. Orville and Wilbur Wright surely knew the dangers they faced. What do you think motivated them to pursue their dreams of flight despite the dangers?

_____

_____

_____

_____

_____

3. Orville and Wilbur Wright borrowed many ideas from earlier aviation pioneers such as Otto Lilienthal and Percy Pilcher. These pioneers contributed to the success of the Wright brothers. Often, the work of others contributes directly to our successes. Can you think of examples in your life where other people have contributed to your achievements?

_____

_____

_____

_____

_____

Name_____ Date_____

CHALLENGES

1. How did the early inventors' attempts at flight resemble that of the Greek mythological character Daedalus?

_____

_____

2. What was the invention of the Montgolfier brothers?

_____

3. Octave Chanute, Otto Lilienthal, and Percy Pilcher were early designers of what device?

_____

4. How were the first successful gliders different in design from earlier attempts?

_____

5. Where did the Wright brothers make their first glider flight?

_____

6. What new parts did the Wright brothers have to design to turn their glider into an airplane?

_____

_____

7. Where did the pilot ride on the Wright brothers' plane?

_____

8. Which Wright brother was the pilot on the first flight?

_____

_____

9. How long did the first flight last?

_____

10. How did the Wright brother's plane look different than those we are accustomed to today?

_____

_____

_____

THE PROGRESSIVE ERA

The progressives were people who desired to reform America. From 1900 to 1917 they worked to end child labor, clean up city slums, stop corruption in politics, and most importantly, to limit the power of corporate trusts. They challenged the powerful interests that were controlling government and preventing "common people" from reaping the benefits of America's growing wealth.

Theodore Roosevelt was one of the progressives working for reforms in business and government.

The central ideal of the progressives was to revolt against organized interests in the name of the common people. Progressive governors such as Robert LaFollete of Wisconsin, Albert Cummins of Iowa, and Hiram Johnson of California promoted reforms in their states. Their goals were to increase the efficiency of the government and achieve social reforms that would benefit the public.

President Theodore Roosevelt was the most famous of all the early progressives. While not as radical in his pursuit of reform as some, he used the presidency as a "bully pulpit" to preach for reform. The term "bully pulpit" was Roosevelt's term for his belief that the president had the unique power to affect public opinion through his speeches. Roosevelt, along with a number of journalists, exposed scandals to the public. Journalists such as Upton Sinclair became known as "muckrakers" for their ability to expose scandals to the public. By effectively building up public opinion in favor of reform, the muckrakers were able to bring about reform through public pressure on politicians.

"Trust-busting" is a term that has become widely associated with the Progressive Era. As America's industrial economy matured, a handful of large corporations came to control a vast amount of the productive capacity and capital of the country. Men such as J.P. Morgan, Andrew Carnegie, and John D. Rockefeller became immensely powerful. Their companies had driven their rivals out of business or bought out their competitors, achieving monopolies or "trusts" for their products. Without competition, their companies were able to charge exceedingly high prices for their products. While forming a trust might have been a good business strategy for the wealthy companies, it clearly was detrimental for the American public. Their influence on government was also great due to their immense wealth, and the American public rightly feared that the government was no longer acting in the public interest but for the interests of the large corporate trusts.

In 1890 Congress had passed the Sherman Anti-trust Act that made the formation of monopolies illegal. For over a decade, however, the government never enforced the legislation. President Roosevelt set out to challenge the power of the trusts using the Sherman Anti-trust Act. He formed a department to investigate and prosecute the worst trusts, and spoke constantly from his "bully pulpit" on the dangers of trusts. More radical progressives were disappointed that Roosevelt did not go further in his trust-busting, but Roosevelt realized that it was impossible to completely unravel all of the trusts, choosing instead to prosecute the worst offenders. Presidents William Taft and Woodrow Wilson followed a similar path after Roosevelt left office.

During the Progressive Era, government took on a new role. For the first time government claimed the right to regulate businesses for the public good. As a result, government grew larger and more powerful, while the political power of large corporations diminished. The public regained faith in a government controlled by the people, rather than one that was controlled by big business.

Name_____ Date_____

POINTS TO PONDER

1. Theodore Roosevelt referred to the presidency as a "bully pulpit" because he believed the president had unique powers to influence public opinion. Roosevelt was the first president to use the office in this way. Do you agree that the president has unique powers to mold public opinion because of the respect people have for the office? Do our current leaders have similar abilities?

_____

_____

_____

_____

2. During the Progressive Era most people learned of the news through newspapers and magazines; radio and television had not yet been invented. Muckraking journalists assumed a prime role of importance in forming public opinion. Do print journalists have the same power today, or has their effect been diminished by television and radio? Have television reporters taken on the roles once occupied by the muckraking journalists?

_____

_____

_____

_____

3. The Progressive Era marked the first time that the American government actively regulated businesses for the benefit of the American public. Government regulations for business have increased dramatically since the Progressive Era. As a result, American business is less competitive with foreign firms, but the American consumers and workers are now well protected. Our government has become substantially larger in the process. Is continued government regulation necessary, or can we allow businessmen more independence by regulating them less?

_____

_____

_____

_____

Name_____ Date _____

CHALLENGES

1. What group of people did the progressives want to protect?

_____

2. What president was an early leader of the progressives?

_____

3. Who were the muckrakers?

_____

_____

4. Why did Theodore Roosevelt refer to the presidency as a "bully pulpit"?

_____

_____

5. Trust-busting was a central activity of the progressives. Why were the monopolies of the trusts bad for the American consumers?

_____

_____

6. What law of 1890 made the formation of monopolies illegal?

_____

7. Name one of the presidents that continued to battle against trusts after Roosevelt left office.

_____

8. What new role did the government take during the Progressive Era?

_____

_____

9. Theodore Roosevelt did not believe it was possible to destroy all of the trusts. What strategy did he pursue instead?

_____

_____

10. How did large companies form trusts (monopolies)?

_____

_____

IMMIGRATION, MIGRATION, AND AMERICAN INDUSTRY

The United States possessed vast mineral resources, aggressive businessmen, and a growing transportation system. What it lacked was the workforce necessary to provide the labor for the mines, factories, and railroads. As late as 1860 the United States had a population of only 40 million. Northern companies soon looked to European immigrants to provide the needed labor.

From 1750 to 1900 Europe's population increased from 140 million to 400 million. Medical advances and better food supplies had reduced infant mortality and increased life spans. The people of Europe had longer and healthier lives,

Thousands of immigrants came to the United States. Many found jobs as low-paid, unskilled laborers.

but they still faced many problems. Jobs were scarce in Europe. Some nations of Europe continued to persecute ethnic and religious minorities. Many Europeans looked to America as a place where they might obtain new economic opportunities and freedoms. Between 1875 and 1915, 25 million Europeans immigrated to the United States. Most came from southern and eastern Europe.

Immigrants often came to the United States after being recruited by agents from American companies. Nearly all of the European immigrants entered American industries as unskilled laborers. They did the hardest, dirtiest, and most dangerous jobs that American-born workers were unwilling to do. Their wages were lower than those of other workers, and they were often discriminated against because of their different customs and inability to speak English. Immigrants tended to live together amongst their countrymen in the poorer parts of American cities. Their lives were difficult, but they persevered in the hope that their children would have better opportunities.

American industry was fueled by European immigration for several decades, but the flow of immigrants ceased in 1914 with the beginning of World War I. Europeans were no longer allowed to leave their countries, and many recent immigrants to America returned to fight for their native lands. American industrialists suddenly found themselves with an acute labor shortage. The Pennsylvania Railroad Company found a solution when it sent company agents to the South to recruit African-American workers. Other northern companies soon followed a similar strategy.

The agricultural southern states had long had a surplus of labor. In the early 1900s the boll weevil had destroyed the cotton crop, causing an economic catastrophe and widespread unemployment in the South. African-Americans were the first to lose their jobs, and they suffered from severe racial discrimination in the South. With northern industries needing labor, African-Americans moved north in large numbers from 1916 to 1930. The movement has become known as the Great Migration. During the Great Migration over one million African-Americans moved to the north, principally to the cities of New York, Philadelphia, Detroit, and Chicago.

African-Americans took the most dangerous and dirty jobs that the immigrants had done before. They were usually forced to accept lower wages, and they did not totally escape from the discrimination they had faced in the South. Some became discouraged and returned to their southern homes, but the migration continued. By the time it ended, one-tenth of the African-American population had moved north in search of better opportunities.

Name_____ Date_____

POINTS TO PONDER

1. We have learned that many people were willing to immigrate from their countries when better opportunities existed elsewhere. They faced the difficulties of adjusting to a new culture and new language, but considered the sacrifices worthwhile because of the opportunities for better-paying jobs. Would you consider immigrating to a different country for a better job? How about moving to a different region of this country, as African-Americans did during the Great Migration? Give reasons for your decisions.

_____

_____

_____

_____

2. Many Europeans also immigrated to America because of the increased freedoms that Americans enjoyed. Some African-Americans moved to the North with the hope of escaping the extreme discrimination they suffered in the South. Are freedom and equality factors that are more important to you than economic opportunity, or is a good job more important? Would you be willing to sacrifice one for the other?

_____

_____

_____

3. Today America still accepts many immigrants, including many who cross our borders illegally. Immigration was clearly a benefit to our economy during the years of industrial growth, because immigrants performed many jobs that people who were born in America didn't want. Today many of our leaders oppose further immigration to our country, claiming that immigrants contribute less than they take. Most economists disagree with this claim. Do you believe that there is still room for more immigrants in our country, or is our population too large already?

_____

_____

_____

Name_____ Date_____

CHALLENGES

1. What were the two reasons given that caused Europe to experience a population increase from 1750 to 1900?

_____

_____

2. Why did many Europeans want to immigrate to America?

_____

_____

3. How did Europeans find out about job opportunities in the United States?

_____

_____

4. Why did European immigration stop in 1914?

_____

_____

5. What group of people did northern companies recruit after 1914 to take the jobs that had been performed by immigrants?

_____

6. What was the cause of the economic catastrophe in the southern states in the early 1900s?

_____

_____

7. What is the name given to the movement of large numbers of African-Americans to the North from 1916 to 1930?

_____

8. Name three of the cities that were listed as principle destinations for African-American migrants.

_____

_____

9. What types of jobs did the immigrants and migrants usually perform in their new homes?

_____

_____

INDUSTRIAL WARFARE: WORLD WAR I

Poison gas was first used in World War I.

When the First World War began in August, 1914, the leaders believed that it would be a short war. The German Kaiser boasted that his troops would return victorious that autumn "before the leaves fall from the trees." The leaders were badly mistaken. Modern warfare proved to be appallingly brutal and costly, and the war did not end until November 1918. More than nine million soldiers were killed, and millions more were wounded.

The causes of the war were complex. The various nations of Europe had been preparing for a major war for many years, and countries allied themselves against each other based on economic competition, national pride, and historic rivalries. All of the major nations of Europe became involved in the war. Germany, Austria, and the Ottoman Empire (Turkey) faced an alliance of England, France, Russia, and several smaller nations. In 1917 the United States also joined the war.

New weapons made World War I different than earlier wars. Vastly improved artillery and the introduction of the machine gun made movement on the battlefield almost impossible. Trench warfare was common, because soldiers dug in to avoid enemy fire. Soldiers were slaughtered by the thousands when they attacked entrenched defenders.

A variety of new and terrible weapons were developed to break the stalemate of the trenches. Factories were converted to produce war material, and engineers worked on developing new weapons. The first of these was poison gas. Poison gas proved to be devastating at first, because it caused men to suffocate or go blind. Chlorine gas was first used by the Germans on January 31,1915, at the battle of the Masurian Lakes and was used regularly by both sides for the rest of the war. Chlorine gas was later replaced by the more deadly phosgene gas and by mustard gas that caused burns to the skin and lungs. However, effective respirators were developed that allowed men to survive poison gas attacks. A second invention was the tank. Experimental tanks were first used by the English in 1916 at the battle of the Somme. The tank's armor protected the crew from rifle and machine gun fire, making attacks on opposing trenches possible. Airplanes were also first used in World War I. The war started only a decade after the Wright brothers' first flight, so the planes of the time were mainly used to spot enemy troop movements. Later planes were armed and were used to bomb enemy troops and supply lines and shoot down enemy planes. World War I also saw the first widespread use of submarines. While submarines took part in some naval battles, their biggest role was to sink enemy supply ships. Germany made the greatest use of submarines and sank hundreds of supply ships. The sinking of the *Lusitania* in 1915 by German submarines angered the American public because 122 Americans were killed; Germany's widespread use of submarine warfare was one reason America joined the Allies in 1917.

The war ended on November 11, 1918, when Germany surrendered. The larger armies and greater industrial output of the Allies finally wore down the German armies. Germany's defeat was official with the signing of the Treaty of Versailles in 1919. Few problems were solved by the war, however, and World War II began just 20 years later.

Name_____ Date _____

POINTS TO PONDER

1. Many of the new weapons, such as poison gas and submarines, changed the way wars were fought. How do you think the appearance of these new weapons changed the experiences of war for the average soldier?

_____

_____

_____

_____

2. In 1914 the leaders of all the warring nations were confident that their side would win a quick victory. Why do you think that they were all so overconfident?

_____

_____

_____

_____

3. World War I was fought at a great cost in money and men, but solved few of the world's problems. Might there be better ways available for nations to resolve their disagreements? What other options are possible?

_____

_____

_____

_____

Name_____ Date_____

CHALLENGES

1. In what years did World War I begin and end?

_____

2. What was the Kaiser's boast?

_____

_____

3. How many soldiers were killed in the war?

_____

4. Name one of the types of poison gas used in the war.

_____

5. What country first used tanks in battle?

_____

6. What country angered Americans by sinking the *Lusitania?* Why?

_____

_____

7. What was the major country on the losing side in World War I?

_____

8. Planes were used for the first time in World War I. What activities did the planes perform?

_____

_____

9. World War I was different than previous wars. How had industrialization changed warfare?

_____

_____

_____

10. What problems did the war solve?

_____

_____

THE RUSSIAN PATH TO INDUSTRIALIZATION

Vladimir Lenin and Joseph Stalin

While nearly all nations followed the same path to industrialization that England had blazed, Russia took a different route. Rather than leave the planning and organization of industrial production to individual businessmen, the government planned the development and growth of Russian industry.

When Russia experienced its communist revolution in 1917, the country was far behind other European nations in industrial output. When the communists took over, they wanted to increase industrial output but weren't sure of how to achieve this goal. Their leader, Vladimir Lenin, died in 1924, and Joseph Stalin gained control of the Communist Party in 1927. He was a brutal dictator who eliminated all opposition to himself within the country but did possess a plan to modernize the nation. His goal was to make the Soviet Union militarily and industrially self-sufficient.

Stalin believed that central control by the government was necessary to quickly industrialize the country. With that in mind, he implemented the first of several Five-Year Plans in 1928. The first Five-Year Plan laid down wages, prices, and production goals that each industry had to meet. It also put forth plans for the construction of new factory cities behind the Ural Mountains, a section of the country that had never possessed any industry. Stalin recognized that the new industries would need thousands of workers. He forced millions of small peasant farmers to join collectivized farms and brought the small peasant plots together to form large farms. Though millions of peasants revolted, the collective farms became a reality, and many peasants moved to the new industrial cities. They provided Stalin with the workforce that industry needed.

Russia began a crash course in industrialization in 1928. The plan was dedicated to heavy industry, especially those that produced steel, coal, electricity, and railroads. New cities such as Magnitogorsk and Stalinsk were created out of barren tundra. The cities were dedicated solely to production of the steel and coal that Russia needed. Much of the work was done by forced labor, but it was also done by enthusiastic young communists who believed they were building a new society. In 1933 the second Five-Year Plan was started, continuing many of the objectives of the earlier plan. Heavy industry was again the focus of the plan, as it was necessary for military production. A third Five-Year Plan followed in 1938 but was interrupted by World War II.

Stalin's Five-Year Plans were successful in industrializing the Soviet Union. By 1938 Soviet workers produced four times as much steel and three times as much coal as in 1928. The new cities of Magnitogorsk and Stalinsk produced more steel in 1939 than all of Russia had in 1914. By 1939 Russian industrial output was the third largest in the world. The Soviet military was modernized.

There were problems, however. Quality control was often poor, and many of the new plants were poorly constructed. Output per worker remained low compared to that of western countries. Thousands of accidents occurred because of long work hours and the rapid pace that was necessary to meet high production goals. Life in the new cities was very difficult, since both housing and food were in short supply. Finally, millions were imprisoned or executed due to Stalin's insistence that dissent was not to be tolerated. His path was the only one allowed.

Name_____ Date _____

POINTS TO PONDER

1. Many of the workers who built Russia's new industrial cities were enthusiastic young communists. They volunteered for the work despite the harsh and dangerous conditions. What do you think motivated these workers?

_____

_____

_____

_____

2. The Soviet government had complete control of the economy through the guidelines of the Five-Year Plan. What kind of problems could total government control create?

_____

_____

_____

_____

3. It is difficult to dispute that Russia made great industrial advances under Stalin. Yet the cost was also high. Millions of people were imprisoned, and the Russian people lived without many of the freedoms we take for granted. How do you judge the experience of Russian industrialization? Was it a success or a failure?

_____

_____

_____

_____

Name_____ Date_____

CHALLENGES

1. What revolutionary group took control of Russia's government in 1917?

_____

2. What leader did Joseph Stalin succeed?

_____

3. What was the name of the scheme that Stalin used to organize the Soviet economy?

_____

4. What type of farms did Stalin create?

_____

_____

5. What was the goal of Stalin's industrial drive?

_____

_____

6. What type of industry did Stalin's plan concentrate on?

_____

_____

7. What were Magnitogorsk and Stalinsk?

_____

_____

8. Stalin's plans were successful in increasing industrial output. What problems were there with Soviet industrialization?

_____

_____

9. How long did Stalin's industrial plans last?

_____

10. What happened to those people who disagreed with Stalin's plans?

_____

_____

FROM CONSERVATION TO ENVIRONMENTALISM

When English colonists first settled in America, the land seemed to offer an unlimited supply of natural resources. Labor, rather than materials, had always been lacking, and for generations Americans used the soil, timber, and mineral resources of the country as if the supply would never be depleted. Rivers and lakes became polluted, forests were destroyed, and animal species were wiped out as American industry grew.

Although industry has been a major source of pollution, recent efforts have been made to control the emission and disposal of harmful substances.

Among the first men to preach against the rapid consumption of America's resources was John Muir. Muir was a tinkerer and inventor who gave up his business pursuits to wander through America's wilderness. He possessed a spiritual reverence for nature and said he felt closest to God when he was wandering through the woods. Muir became an activist, forming the Sierra Club in 1892 to make the public aware of the destruction of the environment. Muir wrote several magazine articles encouraging the government to take a more active role in protecting the environment. President Theodore Roosevelt met with him at Yosemite National Park in 1901.

Theodore Roosevelt was the first national leader to understand that America's resources were limited. Always an outdoorsman, Roosevelt had a sportsman's interest in preserving America's environment and took an interest in the opinion of Muir and other conservationists. Largely because of Roosevelt's leadership, conservation became one of the principles of the Progressive Era. During his presidency Roosevelt called for a program of "rational management" for the nation's resources. He understood that the businessmen of the era preferred to make quick, large profits rather than preserve the country's resources. Only government regulation could dictate rational management of resources, and in 1908 Roosevelt held a White House conference to adopt national policies of natural resource use. While some commercial development of the government lands was allowed, consideration was also given to the preservation of the natural environment.

Conservation gradually disappeared from the public consciousness after Theodore Roosevelt left office, but it again seized the nation's attention while Franklin D. Roosevelt was president. America was suffering from an economic depression, and Roosevelt implemented a program known as the New Deal. Among the New Deal programs was the creation of the Civilian Conservation Corps (CCC) in 1933. The CCC was a program designed partly to provide jobs for the millions of men left unemployed during the depression, but much practical work was done by the agency. The CCC workers planted trees, fought forest fires, and built dams. In 1935 the Soil Conservation Corps was created to promote soil conservation practices among American farmers.

Today Americans have returned to their sporadic concern with conserving natural resources and protecting the environment. Smog, acid rain, and mounting piles of garbage have again brought environmental problems to our attention. The disposal of nuclear waste has presented us with new dilemmas. Taking measures to protect the environment is often expensive. Facing choices between environmental protection and economic growth is never easy. Hopefully, Americans will remain interested in conserving our environment and come to find ways of wisely utilizing our natural resources.

Name_____ Date_____

POINTS TO PONDER

1. By the standards of many people, John Muir was not a success. He did not hold a steady job. He was not wealthy. He had no position of power within his community. Yet Muir influenced the thinking of many people. Would you judge his life to have been a success?

_____

_____

_____

_____

2. Both in the past and at present, there has been a conflict within the environmental movement between those who support "wise use" of resources versus those who advocate preservation (non-use) of resources. What arguments would each group have? Which group do you think has better arguments?

_____

_____

_____

_____

3. Americans have had an irregular interest in conservation over the decades. Presently, environmentalism is again popular. Do you think this concern for the environment will last? Why or why not?

_____

_____

_____

_____

_____

Name_____ Date_____

CHALLENGES

1. What was the attitude of the early Americans regarding our natural resources?

_____

_____

2. What organization did John Muir organize in 1892?

_____

3. Who was the first president who worked to conserve the environment?

_____

4. What was accomplished in the White House Conference of 1908?

_____

_____

5. What was Franklin Roosevelt's program to end the depression called?

_____

6. What activities did workers in the Civilian Conservation Corps perform?

_____

_____

7. What agency was created to solve soil erosion problems during the "Dust Bowl" years?

_____

8. What new waste disposal problem have we had to deal with in recent years?

_____

_____

9. When did John Muir feel closest to God?

_____

10. What was the term for Theodore Roosevelt's program for natural resources conservation?

_____

11. Where did John Muir and Theodore Roosevelt meet in 1901?

_____

_____

THE POSTINDUSTRIAL WORLD

The industrialization of the United States and Europe was essentially complete by the beginning of World War II in 1939. The time period covering the end of the war up to the present day has been given many names over the years. Among the most popular names for our era have been the Atomic Age, the Space Age, the Computer Age, and the Information Age. Future historians will judge which name is most appropriate. In many ways the technological and social changes we have experienced in recent decades have been every bit as revolutionary as those experienced by the English peasants and craftsmen in 1800.

Often called the Space Age, the period after World War II saw great advances in technology—some of which made space travel possible.

New technological developments of the last fifty years have resulted in drastic changes in our society. Agriculture has experienced a rapid growth of production capabilities due to new hybrid plants, chemical fertilizers, and improved production techniques. Synthetic materials and plastics have improved products common to our daily lives. Television has changed the way we entertain and inform ourselves. The power of atomic energy was proven in 1945 when atomic bombs were dropped by the United States on the Japanese cities of Hiroshima and Nagasaki in the closing days of World War II. Since then, while the potential devastation of a nuclear war has haunted civilization, nuclear scientists have found a way to harness atomic energy to produce electricity. The development of jet engines has allowed air travel to become faster, more reliable, and more affordable. Space travel also became a reality, culminating in space flight to the moon in 1969. Finally, computers have revolutionized education, business, and communications.

As always, political changes came with the technological developments. Following World War II the colonial empires of the European nations disintegrated, and new countries emerged in Asia and Africa. Relationships between the industrialized nations also changed as the Cold War followed World War II. The Cold War was a confrontation between the capitalist and communist nations. The United States was the leader of the capitalist nations, and the Soviet Union led the communist nations. Total warfare never broke out, largely because both sides feared the potential destruction of a nuclear war. For several decades, however, tensions between the two sides remained high. The Cold War finally ended in the late 1980s with the economic collapse of communism. Capitalism proved to be the stronger economic system.

A variety of social changes have come with the technological changes. Cities and their suburbs have continued to grow larger. Our wealth has increased, but poverty remains a problem. The health of our economy is no longer tied to industrial production. The "service" and "information" sectors have become an important part of our economy. Industrial jobs have disappeared in many areas that were once the centers of factory production. In recent years people have become more aware of the environmental damage caused by industrialization and have begun to seek solutions to that damage. All of these events have made the last 50 years an era of dramatic change. Though industrial development is no longer the driving force bringing changes to our world, change continues all the same.

Name_____ Date _____

POINTS TO PONDER

1. Several names have been given to the era following World War II. Which do you think is most appropriate? Do you have any other suggestions for a name for our era? Explain your answer.

_____

_____

_____

_____

_____

2. The world has faced several problems in the past 50 years. We have solved some, but many still face us. What do you think is the greatest problem facing us today? Give your reasons.

_____

_____

_____

_____

_____

3. Think back to the beginning of this book and remember what life was like before the Industrial Revolution. What in our lives has improved since that time? What advantages did life before the Industrial Revolution offer?

_____

_____

_____

_____

Name_____ Date_____

CHALLENGES

1. When was the industrialization of the United States and Europe completed?

_____

2. What are two of the popular names that have been given to the age that follows the Industrial Age?

_____

_____

3. In what country were the first atomic bombs dropped in 1945?

_____

4. What happened to the colonial empires after World War II?

_____

_____

5. The Cold War was a conflict between countries advocating what two types of economic systems?

_____

_____

6. What two counties were the most important adversaries in the Cold War?

_____

7. The Cold War ended with the collapse of which side?

_____

8. What other sectors of our economy besides industry have now become important?

_____

_____

9. Several important technological advancements have occurred in the last several years. List four of them.

_____

_____

_____

_____

CONCLUSION

As we have learned, the Industrial Revolution was an event that spanned the lives of many generations. Some historians prefer to speak of an industrial "evolution," pointing out that there was no one great revolutionary event. Rather, what occurred was a sequence of inventions, discoveries, and social movements that make up what we refer to as the Industrial Revolution. Individually each event had a small effect on the world, but taken together the effect was truly dramatic.

The Industrial Revolution brought great power to the nations of Europe and the United States. They gained great advantage from having industrialized first.

Today, scientists and inventors continue to develop new technologies and new ways of doing things in order to improve our lives.

These nations came to dominate the world, largely because of the technological superiority that they enjoyed. Their industries produced more, their populations were wealthier, and their military forces were stronger. Only in recent decades have the other nations of the world begun to catch up.

We have also seen how social changes have resulted from the technological changes. While advances in technology improved people's lives in the long run, the changes often brought problems with them. People struggled to become accustomed to working in factories. The role of children in the workplace took decades to resolve. Pollution still haunts us. These problems and many others were the results of change, and new ideas were needed to attempt to deal with them. In addition to bringing new technologies, the Industrial Revolution caused people to search for new beliefs and new ways of looking at the world.

In summary, when we look at the Industrial Revolution, we see a time when people were forced to cope with breathtaking changes. For centuries before the Industrial Revolution, technological changes had come very slowly. After 1750, however, the technological changes came in rapid succession. They forced drastic changes in the way people worked. The social changes that followed these breakthroughs dramatically changed people's lives. The changes caused many people to suffer, and many saw little hope for the future. The changes brought out both what is noble and what is terrible in humanity. Yet, in the long run, the new technologies benefited our societies.

Today, our world continues to change at a dizzying rate. New ways of doing things occur with regularity. We have become accustomed to constant change, and even anticipate it. Politicians preach it as a virtue to be desired. Change often brings benefits. Yet, there is no denying that change is difficult to deal with. Much like the past, the future will require humanity to solve the problems created by today's world of constant change.

Name_____ Date _____

INDUSTRIAL REVOLUTION CROSSWORD CLUES

Use the following clues to complete the crossword puzzle on page 79. Questions come from information in the narratives.

ACROSS

1. Journalists such as Upton Sinclair were known as _____.

3. Event most feared by coal miners. _____

4. Location of Baldwin Locomotive factory. _____

8. Henry Ford's most successful car. _____

13. Leading coal producing state. _____

14. John _____ was among the early environmentalists.

15. Leader of the American Federation of Labor. _____

19. Name of the first successful locomotive. _____

22. Inventor of the flying shuttle. _____ _____

23. New weapon of World War I. _____

24. Type of poison gas used in World War I. _____

25. Industry where most women found work. _____

DOWN

2. Name of J.P. Morgan's steel company. _____ _____

5. Continent colonized by the Europeans. _____

6. Company town in Illinois. _____

7. Animals used to pull coal carts to the surface in early mines. _____

9. _____ Roosevelt was the first Progressive president.

10. Inventor of the steam engine. _____

11. Karl Marx championed the cause of the _____ .

12. New crop that increased food supply in Europe. _____

16. The _____ Anti-trust Act made formation of monopolies illegal.

17. _____ industry produced cloth before the factory system.

18. The _____ process improved our ability to make steel.

20. Southern crop destroyed by the boll weevil. _____

21. The _____ line allowed Ford to increase production.

INDUSTRIAL REVOLUTION CROSSWORD PUZZLE

Name_____ Date _____

Use the clues from page 78 to complete the puzzle below.

Name_____ Date_____

INDUSTRIAL REVOLUTION
GEOGRAPHY QUIZ

1. From which country did England import most of its cotton? _____

2. Which country became the leading chemical-producing nation?_____

3. Which country was ruled by Joseph Stalin? _____

4. In which city did Thomas Edison build his first electric power plant? _____

5. Which city was the center of textile production? _____

6. Which city had Robert Owen's model factory? _____

7. Which city was the home of Carnegie Steel? _____

8. Which city was the home of the Ford Motor Company? _____

9. Near which town was the Wright brothers' first flight? _____

10. Near which city is the Mesabi iron ore range located? _____

11. Which city was the western end of the transcontinental railroad?_____

12. On which city was the first atomic bomb dropped? _____

13. At what point did the transcontinental rail lines meet?_____

14. Which Asian country was controlled by only 75,000 British troops? _____

15. Across which bodies of water was iron ore transported on its way to steelmaking centers in

the United States? _____

Name_____ Date_____

MAP OF THE UNITED KINGDOM

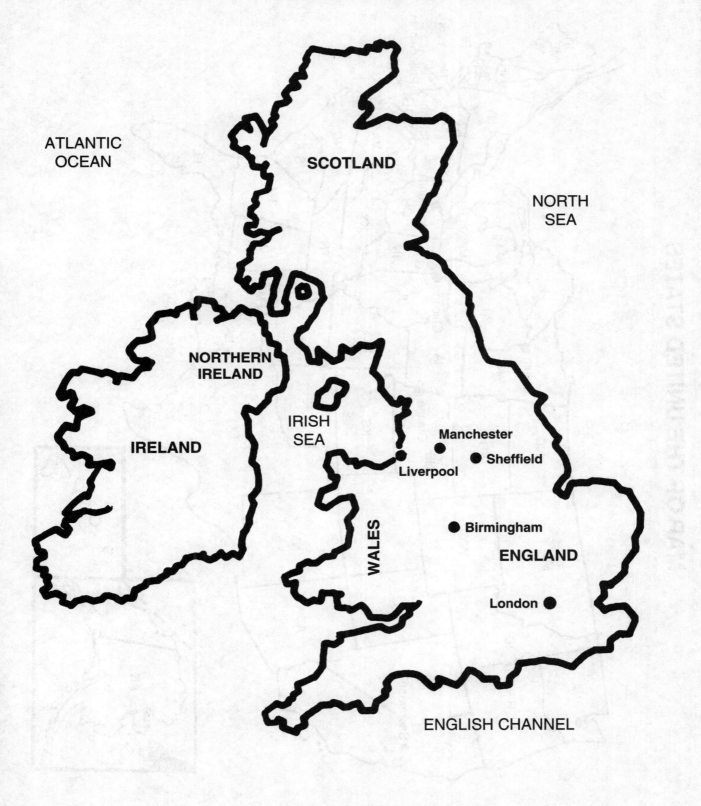

Name_____ Date_____

MAP OF THE UNITED STATES

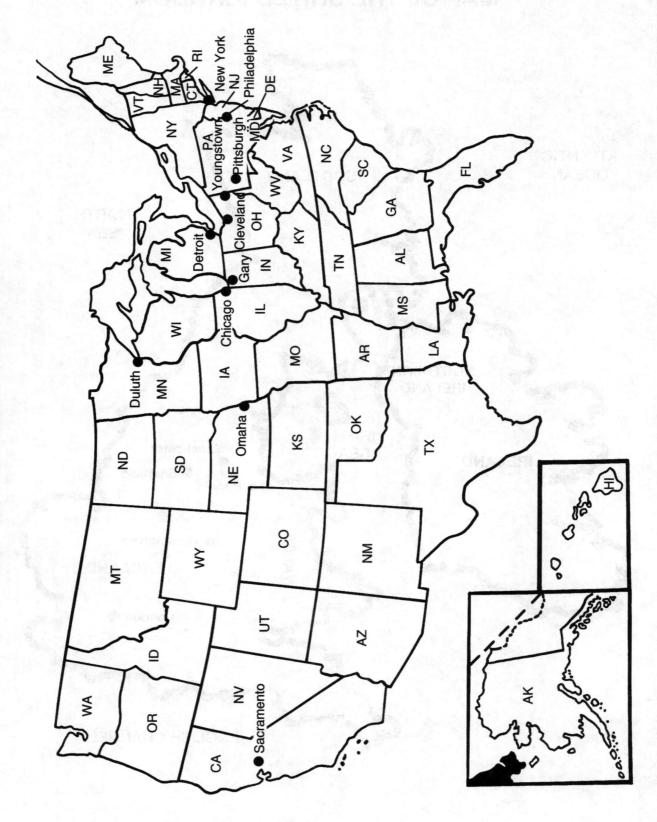

Name_____ Date_____

MAP OF COLONIAL AFRICA

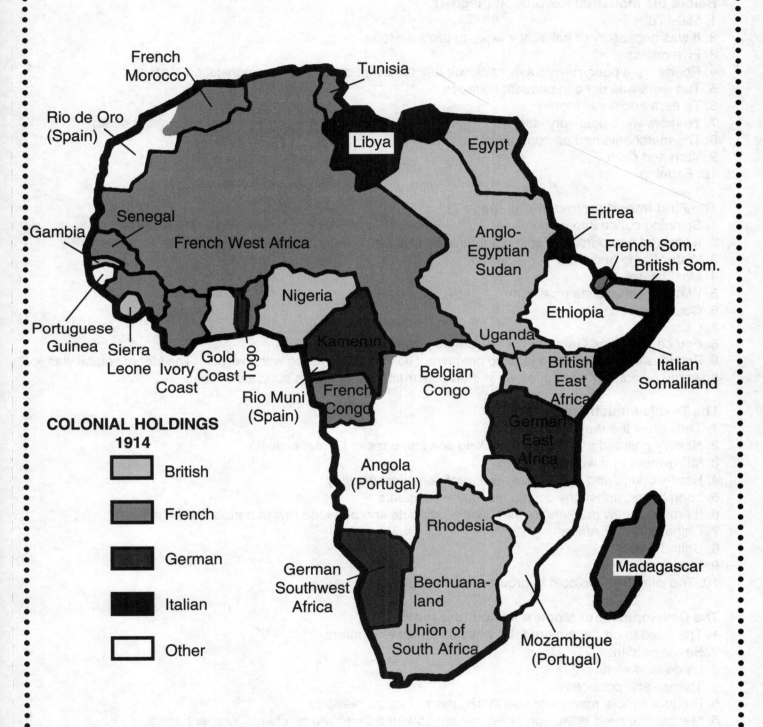

French Morocco

Tunisia

Rio de Oro (Spain)

Libya

Egypt

Gambia

Senegal

French West Africa

Eritrea

French Som.
British Som.

Anglo-Egyptian Sudan

Portuguese Guinea

Sierra Leone

Ivory Coast

Gold Coast

Togo

Nigeria

Kamerun

Ethiopia

Uganda

British East Africa

Italian Somaliland

Rio Muni (Spain)

French Congo

Belgian Congo

German East Africa

COLONIAL HOLDINGS
1914

Angola (Portugal)

Rhodesia

Madagascar

British

French

German Southwest Africa

German

Bechuana-land

Italian

Other

Union of South Africa

Mozambique (Portugal)

ANSWERS

Before the Industrial Revolution (page 4)
1. Mid-1700s
2. It was necessary to have their labor to produce food.
3. Five million
4. Roads were poor, news traveled slowly due to lack of organized communication system.
5. The work was done in peasant cottages.
6. To earn additional money
7. Workers were paid very little, so they could buy goods cheaply and sell them for higher prices.
8. The merchants had no control over the workers.
9. Yarn and cloth
10. Farming

The First Important Inventions (page 7)
1. Spinning cotton into yarn
2. It allowed one person to spin eight threads at once.
3. Water frame and mule
4. Manchester
5. Waterwheel and steam engine
6. Coal mines
7. Coal
8. France, Belgium, Germany, or the United States (any three)
9. Previously, factories were located near rivers so they could utilize water wheels. The steam engine was powered by coal, and factories were then constructed near cheap supplies of coal.

The Textile Industry (page 10)
1. They grew too rapidly.
2. Heavily polluted and crowded, lacking sewers, unpaved streets, slums
3. Mill owners and workers
4. Hard-working and aggressive men, profit-seeking, wealthy
5. Long hours, unhealthy conditions, many accidents
6. It provided new markets for their textile products and provided raw materials for the mills
7. China, India, or Africa
8. United States
9. Manchester
10. The climate is too cold to grow cotton in England.

The Development of Modern Agriculture (page 13)
1. The need to produce more food while using fewer laborers
2. Seven percent
3. Large landowners
4. Turnips and potatoes
5. Produced more meat, matured faster, more disease-resistant
6. Mechanical seed drills, iron plows, steam-powered threshing machines, reapers, tractors
7. Southern United States
8. Fewer farmers and larger farms
9. By using manure from the animals and chemical fertilizers, and by practicing crop rotation
10. The share-cropping system

84

Transportation: the Dominance of Railroads (page 16)
1. James Watt
2. Ships
3. The "Rocket"
4. Coal was needed to fuel the locomotives, iron was needed for the rails and production of the locomotives and boxcars.
5. Cornelius Vanderbuilt, J.P. Morgan, James Hill, or Edward Harriman.
6. Utah
7. Reduced transportation costs for raw materials and finished products
8. Steel rails and bridges, locomotives became more efficient and powerful, electric and diesel locomotives replaced steam engines (any two)
9. On canals and rivers
10. Canals were expensive to dig, and rivers often didn't flow where goods were needed. They were also useless in the winter when the water froze.

Coal and Coal Mining (page 19)
1. To guarantee a cheap and easily obtained source of fuel
2. Railroads and iron production
3. Cave-ins, floods, explosions, black lung
4. To improve mine safety
5. They sorted the coal by size.
6. Steam engines, yes; explosives, no; breakers, no
7. To pull carts of coal to the surface
8. Guided the ponies and donkeys
9. A respiratory disease caused by breathing coal dust
10. Steel industry, chemical industry, power for steam engine, used to heat homes (any two)

Child Labor: Abuses and Reforms (page 22)
1. Learn the skills of the trade
2. They were able to perform some of the simple jobs well and could be paid less money.
3. Long hours, dangerous jobs, poor wages, poor health, no education
4. Child labor was important to the textile industry that was a large part of the English economy.
5. Orphans and children of impoverished parents
6. Limited hours worked, raised wages, prohibited children from performing dangerous jobs
7. Ministers, doctors, and educators
8. Fair Labor Standards Act

Women in the Industrial Revolution (page 25)
1. Worked in the fields and in the house
2. It allowed them to work independently from their families.
3. Textile industry
4. Women filled many of the jobs previously done by children.
5. They paid women less money.
6. They were paid less and not allowed to hold many types of jobs.
7. It was believed that they weren't capable of performing skilled work.
8. Eventually society realized that women were equally capable of performing jobs requiring great skill.

Laissez-faire Economics and Classical Liberalism (page 28)
1. To "let it happen"
2. Adam Smith
3. Through the use of tariffs on foreign products

4. Smith believed the government should not interfere in any way.
5. Provide a military and protect property
6. The iron law of wages
7. Child labor, the growth of slums, poverty
8. Upper-middle class, wealthy
9. They felt that they were being oppressed and called for reforms.
10. England fell behind other nations in developing new technologies.

Karl Marx and the Birth of Socialism (page 31)
1. The current philosophy preached that workers must always live in poverty.
2. With fear and distaste—they were not sympathetic to the suffering of the workers
3. *The Communist Manifesto*
4. The struggle between different classes for control of wealth
5. Factory owners/middle class (bourgeoisie) and workers (proletariat)
6. Proletariat (workers)
7. A violent revolution in which the proletariat would overthrow the bourgeoisie
8. Russia, China, or Vietnam (others acceptable)
9. He predicted that the classes would disappear and everyone would work for the common good.
10. No

Attempts at Reform: Alternate Visions (page 34)
1. New Lanarck, Scotland
2. The town provided a good living and working environment.
3. The members were unable to cooperate effectively.
4. Railroad cars
5. Paved streets; numerous parks; good schools, housing, and transportation; entertainment
6. Alcohol, prostitution
7. Pullman fired workers and cut wages while leaving house rents high.
8. The strike was broken by government troops, and the workers returned to their jobs.
9. He assumed that a pleasant living environment would keep the workers happy even if he cut their wages.

The Growth of Labor Unions (page 37)
1. Bargain collectively for better wages and conditions
2. European unions were often revolutionary, most American unions were not.
3. Better wages and working conditions
4. Knights of Labor
5. Samuel Gompers
6. They were opposed to unions.
7. Pullman or Homestead
8. The right to organize
9. The local unions formed their own rules and negotiated their own contracts.
10. At first the government viewed the unions with suspicion, but later, it accepted unions as a legitimate part of industry.

Imperialism and the Industrial Revolution (page 40)
1. 1870s
2. Africa and Asia
3. It provided the Europeans with superior weapons and the steamship gave Europeans dependable transportation.
4. Economic reasons, national pride, Europe's "civilizing mission," spreading Christianity
5. Rubber, petroleum, copper, cotton, coffee, tea

6. Railroads, warehouses, mines, docks, factories, refineries
7. They resented them.
8. After World War I
9. England, France, Germany, Belgium, the Netherlands (any 3)
10. The 1960s

The Age of Iron and Steel (page 43)
1. It was very expensive to produce.
2. By heating and hammering the pig iron
3. Steel is stronger and more durable.
4. A converter blows hot air through molten pig iron.
5. Open hearth furnace
6. Pittsburgh, Chicago, Gary, Youngstown, or Cleveland (any three)
7. Near Duluth, Minnesota
8. Pennsylvania, Kentucky, or West Virginia (any two)
9. Railroads were used to transport coal to the steel mills, and steamships transported iron ore across the Great Lakes.

Carnegie, Morgan, and the American Steel Industry (page 46)
1. In a cotton mill
2. Pittsburgh
3. Worked to increase production levels; produce a high quality product for a low price; aggressive salesman; drove competitors out of business; vertical integration
4. Becoming involved in the production and control of supplies of raw materials and transportation necessary for the industry
5. Gave it away
6. U.S. Steel
7. It was near large coal and limestone deposits, had a navigable river, many aggressive businessmen
8. 60 percent
9. Income taxes, government regulations, strong unions, and so on.
10. The man who dies rich, dies disgraced.

The Chemical Revolution (page 49)
1. They produced synthetic substances not easily obtainable from nature.
2. England
3. Germany
4. A superior public education system
5. Coal tar
6. Rayon
7. Dynamite, nitroglycerine
8. Bakelite (plastic)
9. Alkalis
10. The textile industry
11. Making paper from wood pulp
12. Synthetic ammonia

Electricity (page 52)
1. Michael Faraday
2. Finding a substance to use as a filament
3. New York
4. General Electric

87

5. The alternating current generator
6. Electric trolleys, trains, and subways
7. Electric wires crisscrossed streets, electric signs were used to advertise, electric lights brightened streets.
8. Brought electric power to rural areas
9. Gas lights and candles
10. The trolley allowed workers to easily commute to their jobs in the city, thus allowing suburbs to grow.

Henry Ford and the Model T (page 55)
1. The internal combustion engine
2. The Ford Motor Company
3. High quality, low price
4. The Model A
5. The Model T
6. The assembly line
7. Five dollars a day
8. 15 million
9. For the first time many Americans were able to afford a car, and the automobile became a central part of Americans' lives.
10. Black
11. The cars were of uniform quality, and replacement parts were easily purchased.

The Wright Brothers (page 58)
1. They utilized flapping wings.
2. The hot air balloon
3. The glider
4. They used fixed wings.
5. Kitty Hawk, North Carolina
6. Propellers and a light, powerful motor
7. On the wing
8. Orville
9. Less than a minute
10. The tail (called an "elevator") faced the front, while the propeller faced the rear. The pilot rode on the wing.

The Progressive Era (page 61)
1. The "common people" or American public
2. Theodore Roosevelt
3. Journalists who exposed scandals
4. He felt that it was a good place to mold public opinion through speech-making.
5. The absence of competition caused prices to rise.
6. Sherman Anti-trust Act
7. William Taft or Woodrow Wilson
8. Regulating business for the public good
9. He elected to prosecute the worst offenders of the Sherman Anti-trust Act.
10. By driving all of their rivals out of business or by buying out their competitors

Immigration, Migration, and American Industry (page 64)
1. Better food supplies and medical care
2. Better jobs, escape religious and ethnic persecution in Europe
3. Company agents from America recruited Europeans.
4. World War I

5. African-Americans
6. The boll weevil had destroyed the cotton crop.
7. The Great Migration
8. New York, Chicago, Detroit, or Philadelphia (any three)
9. They tended to take the dirty, dangerous, low-paying jobs that no one else wanted.

Industrial Warfare: World War I (page 67)
1. It began in 1914 and ended in 1918.
2. That the troops would return home "before the leaves fall"
3. More than nine million
4. Chlorine, phosgene, or mustard gas
5. England
6. Germany. They were unhappy that Americans on board were killed.
7. Germany
8. Primarily to scout enemy troop movements—later planes were armed with bombs and machine guns
9. Warfare became bloodier and more deadly due to the development of new weapons used by massive armies.
10. No problems were solved.

The Russian Path to Industrialization (page 70)
1. The communists
2. Lenin
3. Five-Year Plan
4. Collective farms
5. To achieve industrial and military self-sufficiency
6. Heavy industry
7. New industrial cities
8. Poor construction of plants, poor quality products, many accidents, suppression of dissent
9. Five years
10. They were imprisoned or executed.

From Conservation to Environmentalism (page 73)
1. They thought that supplies would last forever.
2. Sierra Club
3. Theodore Roosevelt
4. National policies on natural resource use were adopted.
5. The New Deal
6. Plant trees, fight forest fires, build dams
7. Soil Conservation Corps
8. Disposal of nuclear waste
9. While walking through the woods
10. Rational management
11. Yosemite National Park

The Post-industrial World (page 76)
1. By the beginning of World War II (1939)
2. Atomic Age, Space Age, Computer Age, Information Age
3. Japan
4. The colonies became independent nations.
5. Capitalism and communism
6. The United States and the Soviet Union

7. Communism collapsed.

8. The service and information sectors

9. Increased agricultural production; increased use of plastics and synthetic materials; television; atomic energy; jet engines; space travel; computers (any four)

Industrial Revolution Crossword Puzzle (page 79)

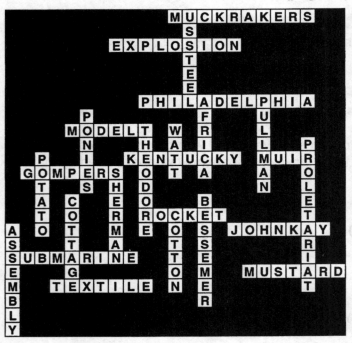

ACROSS
1. Muckrakers
3. Explosion
4. Philadelphia
8. Model T
13. Kentucky
14. Muir
15. Gompers
19. Rocket
22. John Kay
23. Submarine
24. Mustard
25. Textile

DOWN
2. U.S. Steel
5. Africa
6. Pullman
7. Ponies
9. Theodore
10. Watt
11. Proletariat
12. Potato
16. Sherman
17. Cottage
18. Bessemer
20. Cotton
21. Assembly

Industrial Revolution Geography Quiz (page 80)

1. United States
2. Germany
3. Soviet Union
4. New York City
5. Manchester, England
6. New Lanark, Scotland
7. Pittsburgh, Pennsylvania
8. Detroit, Michigan
9. Kitty Hawk, North Carolina
10. Duluth, Minnesota
11. Sacramento, California
12. Hiroshima, Japan
13. Promontory, Utah
14. India
15. The Great Lakes

BIBLIOGRAPHY

Ashton, T.S. *The Industrial Revolution, 1760–1830*. Oxford, England: Oxford University Press, 1948.

Buder, Stanley. *Pullman*. New York: Oxford University Press, 1967.

Cartres, John and David Hey. *English Rural Society, 1500–1800*. Cambridge, England: Cambridge University Press, 1990.

Cashman, Sean. *America in the Age of the Titans*. New York: New York University Press, 1988.

Copland, Ian. *The Burden of Empire*. Melbourne, Australia: Oxford University Press, 1990.

Farber, Eduard. *The Evolution of Chemistry*. New York: Ronald Press Company, 1952.

Floud, Robert and Donald McCloskey. *The Economic History of Britain Since 1700*. New York: Cambridge University Press, 1981.

Freedman, Russell. *The Wright Brothers*. New York: Holiday House, 1991.

Groner, Alex. *American Business and Industry*. New York: American Heritage Publishing Co., 1972.

Hammond, J.L. and Barbara Hammond. *The Rise of Modern Industry*. New York: Harcourt, Brace, and Co., 1926.

Harrison, Alferdteen. *Black Exodus: The Great Migration from the American South*. Jackson, Mississippi: University Press of Mississippi, 1991.

Hobsbawm, E.J. *The Age of Revolution, 1789–1848*. London, England: Wiedenfeld and Nicolson, 1962.

Hobsbawm, E.J. *Industry and Empire*. New York: Pantheon Books, 1968.

Hofstadter, Richard, ed. *The Progressive Movement, 1900–1915*. Englewood Cliffs, New Jersey: Prentice Hall, 1963.

Hofstadter, Richard. *The Age of Reform*. New York: Random House, 1955.

Hudson, John. *The History of Chemistry*. New York: Routledge, Chapman, & Hall, 1992.

Krause, Paul. *The Battle for Homestead*. Pittsburgh, Pennsylvania: University of Pittsburgh Press, 1992.

Lacey, Robert. *Ford: The Men and the Machine*. Boston: Little, Brown, and Company, 1986.

Landes, David. *The Unbound Prometheus: Technological Change and Industrial Development in Western Europe from 1750 to the Present*. New York: Cambridge University Press, 1969.

Lindsey, Almont. *The Pullman Strike*. Chicago: University of Chicago Press, 1964.

Lipset, Seymour. *Unions in Transition*. San Francisco: ICS Press, 1986.

Livesay, Harold. *American Made: Men Who Shaped the American Economy*. Boston: Little, Brown, and Co., 1979.

Marks, Carol. *Farewell—We're Good and Gone: The Great Black Migration*. Bloomington, Indiana: Indiana University Press, 1989.

Mathias, Peter. *The First Industrial Nation: An Economic History of Britain, 1700–1914.* New York: Methuen, 1969.

Mokyr, Joel, ed. *The Economics of the Industrial Revolution.* Rowen and Littlefield, 1985.

Moolman, Valerie. *The Road to Kitty Hawk.* Alexandria, Virginia: Time-Life Books, 1980.

Nevins, Allan. *Ford: The Times, the Man, the Company.* New York: Charles Scribner's Sons, 1954.

Nye, David. *Electrifying America: Social Meanings of a New Technology.* Cambridge, Massachusetts: MIT Press, 1990.

O'Brien, Patrick and Roland Quinault, ed. *The Industrial Revolution and British Society.* New York: Cambridge University Press, 1993.

Palmer, R.R. and Joel Colton. *A History of the Modern World Since 1815.* New York: Alfred A. Knopf, 1984.

Snyder, Louis, ed. *The Imperialism Reader.* Princeton, New Jersey: D. Van Nostrand Company, 1962.

Taylor, Philip. *The Industrial Revolution in Britain: Triumph or Disaster?* Boston: D.C. Heath, 1958.

Teale, Edwin, ed. *The Wilderness World of John Muir.* 1976.

Toynbee, Arnold. *The Industrial Revolution of the Eighteenth Century in England.* London: Longmans, Green and Co., 1913

Ulam, Adam. *Stalin, The Man and His Era.* Boston: Beacon Press, 1973.

Warne, Colston, ed. *The Pullman Boycott of 1894.* Boston: D.C. Health and Company, 1955.

Wiebe, Robert. *The Search for Order, 1877–1920.* New York: Hill and Wang, 1967.

Winter, J.M. *The Experience of World War I.* New York: Oxford University Press, 1989.

Young, Brigadier, ed. *The Marshall Cavendish Illustrated Encyclopedia of World War I.* New York: Marshall Cavendish, 1986.

Youngs, J. William. "John Muir and the American Wilderness" in *American Realities: From Reconstruction to the Present.* Boston: Little, Brown, and Co., 1981.